BARRON'S PARENTING KEYS

KEYS TO PREPARING AND CARING FOR YOUR SECOND CHILD

Meg Zweiback, R.N., M.P.H., C.P.N.P.

Assistant Clinical Professor
University of California,
San Francisco

BARRON'S

All inquiries should be addressed to:
Barron's Educational Series, Inc.
250 Wireless Boulevard
Hauppauge, New York 11788

Library of Congress Catalog Card No. 91-6571

International Standard Book No. 0-8120-4698-6

Library of Congress Cataloging-in-Publication Data

Zweiback, Meg.
  Keys to preparing and caring for your second child /
    by Meg Zweiback.
    p. cm.—(Barron's parenting keys)
  Includes bibliographical references.
  ISBN 0-8120-4698-6
  1. Second-born children. 2. Parenting. 3. Brothers and
sisters.
  I. Title. II. Series.
HQ777.22.Z84 1991
649'.143—dc20   91-6571
                                        CIP

PRINTED IN THE UNITED STATES OF AMERICA
1234 5500 987654321

CONTENTS

INTRODUCTION

Sibling relationships? Sibling rivalry? Which two words express your thoughts as you plan your family? If you are thinking about having a second baby, if you are already pregnant again, or if you are busy adjusting yourselves and your older child to a new arrival, you are most certainly thinking about your children's reactions to each other. There is no question that your new baby will bring changes to your family, some welcome and some not. There is also no question that along with the joys of a new baby will come problems, some predictable and some not. In this book, you will find out how to help your growing family cope with change. You will also learn how to use the inevitable problems as opportunities to grow and develop together into a stronger unit.

During my sixteen years as a nurse practitioner and family consultant I have met with thousands of families through my practice and the many parent workshops I lead. Parents who are having a second baby, I have found, first worry about how the arrival of their new baby will affect the first child. After the new baby arrives, the parents begin to worry about how the two children interact with each other, and how the siblings' relationship affect the whole family. This book is organized to help you deal with your concerns in the order that they occur.

In the first half of the book, Keys 1 through 25, you will find guidelines to planning your family, getting through your second pregnancy and birth, and adjusting to the new baby's arrival. You will find ideas for ways to talk to your first child and help him to have the best possible reaction to this important event. You will also find suggestions for yourselves, for you as parents have your own worries and needs at this time. Even if your second baby has already arrived, you should read this section. You will gain a greater understanding of what your child's experiences have already been, and you may find ways that you can still assist him in feeling positive about pregnancy and childbirth.

The Keys in the second half of this book will be helpful to you whether you have one child, two, or even more. In these Keys, you will find guidelines for helping your family meet the challenge of being the loving, supportive foundation each of your children needs to become a successful adult. The relationship between your children, and how you as a parent help or hinder that relationship, is very important. But equally important is the way in which your whole family nurtures one another, and how each child learns from you to cope with conflict.

Parents sometimes feel that sibling rivalry will be their major problem if they have more than one child. It is certainly true that in families where siblings spend much of their time fighting and hurting one another parents may believe that if their children got along better the family's problems would be solved. But this kind of rivalry doesn't have to occur.

Often, what parents call "sibling rivalry" is simply the conflict that comes from the inability of young children to behave like mature adults. It takes a long time for children to learn about sharing, about settling disagreements by talking rather than fighting, and about accepting that people can be different from one another without being "better." These are the skills that parents must teach their children, but children do not learn in a vacuum. They learn about getting along with others through their own experience, by trial and error. If we label their many errors "sibling rivalry," as though these normal problems are something pathological, then we deny our children their right to learn how to do better. Every time your children are together, they are learning. As you help them to get along at home, you are teaching them to get along in the world.

When sibling conflict is constant, it may be that the sibling relationship is a mirror for other problems within a family. Sometimes, the problem is simply a lack of time spent with the parents. If a child feels she never gets enough attention from the people she loves most, she may take out her anger on the sibling whom she perceives as taking too much of what they both need. Other times, the problem is that the family is stuck in certain patterns of relating and communicating with one another, patterns so familiar that no one realizes they aren't working. Sometimes, sibling conflicts arise because one or both children have a low feeling of self-worth, and the unhappiness the child feels emerges as angry behavior.

All of these sibling problems can be helped by parents who from the beginning work together to foster healthy relationships among all family members. The Keys that follow will show how you can improve your ability to help yourselves and your children to manage conflict, to communicate better, and to enjoy the time you spend together. As you develop your own skills as a parent, you will be able to help your children become the friends and allies you want them to be.

1

SHOULD WE HAVE A SECOND CHILD?

For many parents, the decision to have more than one child is automatic. Both parents can agree that a family is composed of two (or more) children, and the only question is when the second child will come along.

Other families are not as sure about whether to expand beyond one child. There are many reasons that parents may hesitate. Raising children is expensive, and parents may not feel that they can provide well enough for more than one. Raising children takes time, and some parents who work outside the home may feel as though they don't have the time to care for more than one child. For some parents, the first child may have been difficult to conceive or to carry to term, and the emotional costs of trying again may seem to be too much to take on.

It's not uncommon for one parent to be ready for a second child whereas the other parent is feeling ambivalent or negative about having more than one. It's important to talk and listen to each other when you have these different expectations. The decision to have more than one child may seem like a rational one, but it is also an emotional decision. The reasons that one parent may give for having, or not having, another baby may be only part of the whole picture. So as you read the Keys in this section, remember that there is no "right" decision or plan for a family, *except* the decision that both parents can support together.

Of course, no matter how carefully you plan, you may not wind up with the family you thought you would have. You may become pregnant unintentionally, or you may have difficulty becoming pregnant when you want to. In these situations, it's even more important for parents to be able to talk to each other openly about any doubts or worries concerning their future family.

2

~~~~~~

PLANNING FOR THE NEXT CHILD

A s you plan for your second child, take the time to think about what it will be like to be the parents of two. No matter how much you and your partner agree about wanting more children, you probably have some different expectations about how a second child will affect your lives.

Here are some questions to ask yourselves now, whether you are just thinking about another baby or are already pregnant. Even if your second baby has already been born, these questions may be interesting for you to answer together.

How do you expect your lives to change once your second child is born? Consider the following:

- Do both parents take care of your child on a daily basis, or does one parent do more of the routine care? Do you expect this proportion to change after the new baby is born? Sometimes a mother who has been working outside of the home is planning to stay at home for a while after the new baby comes. Do you plan to change the way that you share housework or child care if one parent is at home all of the time? These are issues that can be great sources of conflict later if you don't think about them now.

- How will a second child affect your family finances? Do you have enough earnings or savings to adjust to the expenses of a new baby? Don't forget to look at the additional costs of health insurance and child care. Although most parents manage to adjust their finances to the degree needed to have the children they want, it's always better to be realistic in your plans.

• What are your expectations for how your two children will relate to each other? Do you have a fantasy of how siblings should behave? Do you think that your fantasy is likely to be true? Sometimes parents have a mental picture of a perfect sibling relationship that could never exist, no matter how compatible their children turn out to be. Recognizing a fantasy for what it is will help you adjust more easily to the relationship your children create for themselves.

• What kind of memories do you have from your own family? Were you an only child or did you have siblings? Were you older or younger than they were, and were they the same sex or the opposite sex? Do your memories affect the way you want your children to relate to each other? Many parents are surprised to find out how much their own childhood memories differ from their spouses', and how much these memories can affect the way they plan to raise their own children. Differences can usually be worked out, but they have to be recognized first.

• As you ask yourselves these questions, don't feel that you have to come up with the answers right away. Your answers may change as you think about them. You may find that the answers you give before your second baby is born are different than the answers you might give later on. As you probably remember from your experience with your first baby, reality is almost always different from expectations!

3

SPACING CHILDREN

There was a time when parents did not consider what the ideal spacing of their children should be. That time, of course, preceded the advent of reliable family planning methods, as well as the awareness that relationships between children could be affected by the timing of their births. It is now common for parents to be told that there are ideal times to have children and that the interval between the first and second child is critical to the healthy psychological development of each. Some parents may feel that their children do or do not get along well because their birth dates are either close or far apart. These parents may be correct in talking about their own families, but there are no definitive findings to support the notion that there is an optimal time for families in general to have a second child. Family relationships are affected by many different factors, and the spacing of your children may not be as significant as other factors.

However, there are some differences in the way you will be able to care for your children that are influenced by their ages and spacing, so you may want to consider the advantages and disadvantages of different intervals. Even if you are already pregnant or if your second baby has been born, the information in this key will give you some ideas about what to expect.

Nine to Eighteen Months Apart. If your children are born less than a year and a half apart, you will be raising two children whose needs will frequently overlap. The older sibling will still have many "babylike" needs for comfort, attention, and nurturing, when the new baby arrives. The older child will not have the ability to understand the differences between her age and the baby's, and may be confused and upset by her sudden displacement. The older child will also be at the stage of development where she is testing her independence from her parents, especially her mother. You can expect her to act very clingy at times, perhaps alternating with aggressive behavior towards you or others. If both parents or other extended family members are available to help with the work of the two little ones, and if mom is careful to make time for big sister alone every day, this spacing will be hard work but manageable.

As the children get older, they will have the advantage of being close enough in age to be excellent playmates. Nevertheless, the younger child will probably always be striving to keep up with the older one, while the older one may often feel that the younger sibling has it much easier. These feelings can result in too much competition, and parents will have to resist making comparisons or being drawn into conflicts. (See Key 36.) Despite the competition, many adult siblings report that they feel an intense closeness to the brother or sister born with this short interval, a closeness that persists throughout their lives.

Perhaps the most important factor to consider in this kind of spacing is the mother's health. When a woman becomes pregnant within a year of giving birth, her body has not completely recovered, and the demands of her first baby may prevent her from getting the rest she needs during the second pregnancy. When babies are spaced this closely, there is also a higher rate of complications for both mother and second child. It is extremely important that a mother planning this spacing get regular obstetrical care and be carefully screened for risks to herself and the baby. If the pregnancy and birth go well, she will need a great deal of help at home during her recovery in order to cope with the challenges ahead.

Eighteen Months to Three Years Apart. If your children are spaced between eighteen months and three years apart, they will have the age difference that is most common in this country. There are many advantages to this spacing. The older child will have some understanding of what you are saying to him and will be able to express himself better, especially as he nears the age of three. Although a two-year-old still has many "babylike" needs for care, probably including diaper changing, he is able to wait for his needs to be met. He is most likely also on a fairly predictable schedule and should be sleeping through the night (although he may begin waking up once the baby arrives). He has the ability to play by himself for short periods and is at a stage of development where he wants to help out and imitate his parents. Although he will certainly feel left out and resentful at times because of the new baby's demands, he can understand that the baby is smaller than he is. Parents will be able to deal with the older child by talking to him and listening to him. They should expect to see a certain amount of clingy behavior and regression that will appear and reappear throughout the younger child's infancy.

This spacing is popular with parents. The parents are accustomed to dealing with the demands of a young child, and the new baby may seem to require less attention than their toddler. The children are close enough in age to eventually be able to play together and share activities, yet far enough apart to be able to get individualized attention from their parents. They will probably not be in the same preschool class, thus making competition less intense. Because the spacing is so common, it is quite possible that your family will know other families with two children similar in age to yours. Parents and children can get support and companionship by forming friendships with these families. Even in the beginning, the older child is likely to know other children his own age who have new babies at home.

Even though this spacing is popular, most of the books that are written for children whose mothers are expecting a baby are geared to the older children. Young children in general do not learn best from books. The younger your child is, the more he has to be able to see or touch, as well as listen, in order to learn. Therefore, most of the preparation and teaching your child needs will come directly from you in the way you care for both baby and big brother.

Three to Five Years Apart. Some child-rearing experts have suggested that the ideal time to space children is three to four years apart. Their reasoning is that when the older child has reached this age she is able to talk well and to understand and reason in a limited way, and consequently does not need nearly as much caretaking time as the younger child does. These are valid reasons to recommend this interval, but this spacing may not be practical for other considerations. There is no research to support the idea that this spacing results in sibling relationships that are better than those between children spaced more closely.

Some parents worry that a child who has been the one and only for three or more years will feel "dethroned" by the arrival of a new baby. It is certainly true that becoming an older sibling can mean that the exclusive relationship your older child has had with you will be ended. However, when your child turns three she is also at an age when she is developing the skills and desire to have her social needs met by people other than her parents. At three, your child is ready and eager to play with other children, to go to nursery school, and to play independently. Even if you did not have a second child, the exclusive relationship you had with your older child would be changing. For parents, having a second child at this time may make it easier for them to allow their first child to develop her independence.

This is not to say that a child in this age group will not need your help in adjusting to the new baby. Rather, at her age she has more skills to help her cope with change, and more interests to distract her from the shift in her parents' attention. Children in this age group are ready and willing to learn about how to get along with others, including members of their own family. Perhaps the most important element in managing the older child between three and five is to recognize her need for interaction with and attention from her parents. Your child will prefer positive attention, but if she learns that the only attention she can count on is the negative attention she gets from misbehavior, you will find that she will provoke you much of the time. It's important to reserve time every day for your older child that can be pleasant for both of you.

The biggest disadvantage of this spacing is that your children will have different abilities and attention spans for many years, and there will be many times when you will have to do separate activities with each of them. Some parents enjoy the differences, feeling that it helps them to see their children as individuals and allows the children to more easily develop different interests.

Five or More Years Apart. If your children are born more than five years apart, they will in many ways be growing up separately from each other. Competition, while still present, will be less of a problem than with any other spacing. They will always have different friends, activities, and probably schools. However, they can still develop a close and loving relationship, and the older sibling is likely to enjoy the role of being a little parent some of the time. Although most parents do not usually plan this kind of spacing, those who wind up with it often report that they can enjoy their second child enormously because they have had time to relax as their first child has become more independent. And many parents also comment that it is a relief not to have to worry about financing two college educations at the same time!

4

ARE SECOND CHILDREN EASIER?

Many parents believe that their second child is easier to care for than their first child. There are a number of reasons why they may experience the second child as easier, some of which have to do with the parents and some to do with the child. However, it is not always true that the second child is easier, and parents should be aware that in some cases she may even be more difficult to care for!

The factors that make a second child easier or more difficult can be divided into two categories: parent and child.

Parent Factors. Second-time parents have mastered most of the caretaking tasks of child rearing. They know how to feed a baby, diaper her, bathe her, and help her to sleep. They recognize that the baby will change and that they must adjust their care as she changes and grows. Parents have already modified their daily lives to include many hours of child-centered activity, and have begun to work out styles of parenting that feel comfortable for them. Having leapt the hurdle of becoming first-time parents, they will be able to take the next jump in stride, knowing what will be expected of them.

Because parents are more experienced the second time, they often are able to relax and enjoy the second baby more. The same behaviors that caused them to worry with number one are now seen as normal. Therefore, the baby may not be any easier to care for, but the parents don't perceive her as difficult. The parents' calmer response to the baby may even help her to settle herself more because she is not being over-stimulated by her well-meaning but anxious parents!

Child Factors. Any parent of more than one child knows that from the moment of birth, babies are different. Some babies have more of an inner rhythm and predictability than others. A second time baby who has this innate regularity will follow a schedule sooner because family life is already somewhat structured. Babies also love to watch older children play. The second baby may seem to be content and amused for much longer periods, because she has the entertainment of her older sibling's activities. Second children are often easier because their cues are more quickly understood by their more experienced parents, and as these cues are reinforced, they learn to communicate their needs more quickly. Perhaps most importantly, second babies grow up learning by observing their older sibling's behavior. They learn what works with their parents and what does not, simply by watching. They may not need to do as much testing to find out what the limits are in the family.

Second Children Are Different. Whether your second child is easier or not, she will most certainly be different from number one. Different does not mean opposite, however. Both children will benefit if you can keep from labeling them "easy" or "difficult," even if you as parents sometimes wish you had known as much the first time as you do now.

5

~~~~~~

TELLING NUMBER ONE

Parents are sometimes advised to delay telling the older child about the expected new baby. The most frequently given reason is that the older child has little ability to comprehend time and that the nine months of pregnancy will seem like forever to him. It is true that young children don't understand time very well. For most children under five, the concept of a baby due next year is hard to imagine. However, there will be many changes during the nine months of pregnancy that may affect your child's daily life, and for this reason you may want to tell him that you are expecting a baby. Here are some options about when to tell and what to say.

Some parents choose to keep their pregnancy a secret from all but the closest friends and family until the mother is about three months along. This choice is particularly common among parents who have experienced a miscarriage in the past. If you want to keep the news about the pregnancy to yourselves, it's best not to tell your child, since he can't be expected to understand or follow your wishes to keep a secret. However, you may need to reconsider your decision if Mom is feeling very tired or nauseated, as is common during the first trimester. Your first child will be affected by his mother's state of well-being and by her ability to take care of him. If he senses that his mother is sick, but that no one is willing to talk to him about it or that there is a secret about her that he doesn't know, he may become anxious or fearful. It would be better for him to be told that she is pregnant than to have him worry.

Whether you tell your older child early or late, don't feel that you have to make a big announcement. It's best just to tell your child at a quiet time, perhaps when you are out for a walk or driving in the car. A young child will have difficulty comprehending the idea of a baby being born in the future. Since he learns best from direct experience, talking more about the baby will not make him understand more. He really only needs to know two things: You are going to be having a baby, but the baby will not be born for a while. If your child is under two, he may act as if he hasn't even heard you. A child from two to three may look interested or even ask where the baby is now. Three-year-olds may ask questions based on their previous experience with babies, and it can be helpful to them if you begin to point out women who are pregnant or show them families with new babies.

Here are some ways you can tell your young child about the new baby you are expecting:

"We're going to have a new baby in our family. The baby is growing inside mommy now, but it won't be born for a long time." You can tell your child that mommy is "pregnant" and that that word means "going to have a baby."

If mom has been tired or feeling sick, you can add, "Sometimes when mommies are pregnant they don't feel well and they have to lie down and rest a lot. Sometimes they get sick to their stomachs. There's nothing to worry about and she'll be feeling better soon. If she isn't feeling well, there will always be someone to take care of you."

Some children will ask questions now, but others will seem to ignore you. Your child may even begin talking about the baby weeks or months later as though continuing the previous conversation. (See Key 9.)

Although there is very little that you need to tell your child now about the new baby, there are some phrases you should *avoid* using:

- "We think you are so wonderful that we've decided to have another baby"—A child may think, "If I'm so wonderful, why do they need another one?"
- "We're going to have another baby so that you will have a brother or sister to play with"—it will be years before the younger child will be a true playmate, and you will set up an unrealistic expectation.
- "Just because we are having a new baby doesn't mean we will love you less"—Your child may not be able to imagine that he could be loved less, but if you introduce the idea he may start to worry.

If your child is quiet, don't push the subject of the new baby at all. He will take in the information in his own way at his own pace, and reminding him or pushing him to react will not help.

6

THE SECOND TIME IS DIFFERENT

The first time that you were pregnant, every change that you experienced, physical or emotional, was new. You were probably fascinated by the idea of life growing inside you. If you had unpleasant symptoms such as morning sickness or nausea or extreme fatigue, you may have found that your excitement about being pregnant helped you to cope. When you felt good, you probably spent time imagining the wonderful, probably perfect baby you were going to produce. In your last trimester, you may have thought a lot about getting through labor and delivery, but you probably didn't worry about handling the next eighteen years of being responsible for a child!

So here you are, pregnant again. The pregnancy will be in some ways the same and in other ways different. Almost all second-time parents say that the biggest difference for them in the second pregnancy is that this time they are primarily dealing with the needs of their first child, rather than their own needs. That means that they sometimes don't have the time or energy to worry, but it also can mean that they don't have the time to take care of themselves, physically or emotionally. The following Keys will help you to look at your own needs during pregnancy as well as those of your first child.

7

~~~~~~

PHYSICAL CHANGES FOR MOM

The second pregnancy is usually very different from the first. For one thing, the monthly changes in your body aren't as interesting when the experience is no longer new. In addition, second pregnancies are sometimes more uncomfortable. The muscles of your abdomen and pelvis have been stretched, and your muscle tone will be less firm. Most women find that with regular exercise they can regain their tone, but they have to keep up their effort or the abdominal muscles will stretch again. The fibers of your uterus have been stretched too, and these factors combined may cause your belly to grow faster and protrude more rapidly than it did the first time, regardless of your weight gain. The stretching of the blood vessel walls in a second pregnancy can lead to distended or varicose veins, sometimes felt as aches in your legs even if the varicosities are not visible.

You'll probably feel the baby move earlier than you did the first time, but you may also be more sensitive to his rolls and kicks. The ligaments that support the uterus may be more relaxed than before, and you may feel more pressure in your pelvic area and on your bladder. As the baby grows and space gets tighter, your bladder capacity will get smaller. If the muscles of the pelvic floor are weak, you may find that you are leaking urine, especially when you laugh or sneeze.

Some women find that they gain more weight during their second pregnancies, probably more for psychological reasons than for physical ones. Increased weight gain can put more stress on a pregnant woman's back. As your abdomen and uterus grow, your center of gravity shifts forward. To overcome this forward pull, you may throw back your head and shoulders, causing your spine to curve. Over time, this posture will cause your lower back to ache, particularly at the end of the day.

The second pregnancy is often more tiring than the first one, not just because you're older but because you also have a child who probably won't let you rest when you need to. Taking good care of yourself physically pays off in the long run, but can be a challenge when your first child demands your time and attention.

To minimize the stresses and discomforts of a second pregnancy, try the following:
- Follow a simple but well-balanced diet, including all four food groups, but minimizing the amount of fat in your food. Be sure to take a prenatal vitamin supplement with iron. Don't worry about elaborate meals. The plain food you're probably feeding your child will be just as good for you.
- Get regular exercise to increase your overall fitness and keep your weight gain down. Exercise will improve your blood circulation and help prevent swollen ankles and feet, varicose veins, and hemorrhoids that result from blood pooling in your lower extremities. A daily walk is ideal, and if you're pushing a toddler in a stroller you'll get an even better workout.
- Do "Kegel" exercises to strengthen the pelvic floor muscles that support your internal organs and prevent urinary leakage. You can locate the muscles by contracting your vaginal area as if you are trying to stop the flow of urine. Hold the contraction for one second, and then relax. Repeat fifteen times. Try to do a set of these several times each day. Some

women remind themselves by "Kegeling" whenever they stop at a red light! Do these exercises now and after the baby is born for faster healing and continued muscle tone.

- Wear comfortable clothing, including a supportive bra. If your legs ache at all, it's advisable to wear support hose and to sit whenever possible with your legs and feet elevated in order to decrease the pooling of blood in the veins of your legs.
- Keep your back strong by resisting the temptation to slouch with your belly out. Instead, tuck your buttocks in and straighten your shoulders. If you need to bend down, bend your knees and squat rather than stoop over.
- Try to schedule a daily rest; for most women it's a physical necessity. It's often more practical to lie down (on your left side to promote better circulation of blood to your uterus) for several 10- to 15-minute stretches than to take a longer rest. You'll have more energy in the long run if you take the time to rest now.

8

^^

EMOTIONAL CHANGES FOR MOM AND DAD

Just as the mother experiences physical changes during her pregnancy, both parents will also experience emotional changes. But because emotional changes are not as easily recognized as physical ones, some couples aren't aware that what they are feeling is a normal reaction and adjustment to pregnancy. During the second pregnancy, you may experience some feelings that you had the first time, but you may not remember having them! You are also likely to have emotional reactions that come from being a parent already. In this Key you will read about some emotions that parents express during pregnancy. Some may seem familiar to you, others may not, because there is no "typical" way to feel.

One feeling frequently expressed by parents during the second pregnancy is,"How can we take care of a second child and still give enough love and attention to our first?" Some parents worry that they won't be able to love another baby as much as they love the first one. Other parents feel that they *will* love the second baby as much, but worry that the first child will be devastated by having to share this love. Both parents, but especially fathers, may have the very concrete worry: "How will we be able to afford a second child?" It seems as though the second child's birth drives home the meaning of the lifelong financial as well as emotional responsibilities that parents have already assumed with their first child. Although there is no simple way to deal with these worries, it is sometimes reassuring to recall the time when you had no children at all. Did you ever think, at that time, that you would be able to love and care for even one child the way you do now? Most parents find that after the second child arrives and begins to be a real part of their family they are able to expand their capacity for giving (and paying!) just as they did the first time.

Another emotion that some mothers express is a feeling of withdrawal from their first child that may increase as the pregnancy draws to a close. The pregnant woman starts to need more and more time alone, partly for rest, but partly to care for herself psychologically. A mother may start to feel guilty as she is torn between having time for herself and being with her child or her husband. It's helpful to have some quiet time alone whenever you can. If you are with your child, you can plan an activity that doesn't demand too much interaction but can be satisfying to both of you. Taking a walk, reading, or even just watching "Mr. Rogers" together can be a way to conserve your energy.

Another anxiety some second-time pregnant mothers experience is the feeling of being overwhelmed by work and responsibilities. Since this is your second child, however, you probably have a more realistic, rather than idealistic, idea of the time it takes to care for a new baby. If your first baby was colicky or didn't sleep much, you may be fearing a repeat performance. If you are anticipating a return to work, you may be wondering how you will ever get anything done. The more you worry, the more you may feel out of control. One way to cope with your worries is to make plans for the postpartum period, using the ideas in these Keys for guidance.

One of the biggest problems for a second-time parent is finding someone else to talk to. The first time, you can get support from friends, family, and the many professionals who are trying to help you learn about parenting. Second-time parents often feel ignored, as though everyone assumes that they no longer need advice or support. You can overcome this feeling by letting others know that you would appreciate their assistance, and that just because you've been through this before, you're still "first-timers" at being "second-timers"!

9

‸‸

EXPLAINING PREGNANCY AND CHILDBIRTH TO YOUNG CHILDREN

Parents often worry about how to explain pregnancy and childbirth to a young child. How much should you say? What words should you use? Does a preschooler need to know the "facts of life"? Talking to your child is really much easier than you might think, and the ideas in this Key will help you to respond to any questions your child may ask.

Many children are not interested in how a baby is conceived or born. They accept Mom's pregnancy as one more event (like many others) in their lives that is interesting only if it directly affects them. Their questions, if any, are simple. The following anecdote illustrates this point: A little boy named Joey asked his parents, "Where did I come from?" Joey's parents launched into a detailed explanation of sexuality, conception, pregnancy, and birth, while Joey listened attentively. When they finally paused, he remarked, "That's pretty interesting, but Billy next door just told me that he's from Chicago, and I want to know where did *I* come from?"

Clearly, the first principle of answering any questions from your child is to make sure you know what he or she is asking you. It's often helpful first to ask, "Tell me more about what you want to know," or "What do you think?" Sometimes a question about pregnancy and birth is simply a request for an explanation of Mommy's expanding belly, or an expression of bewilderment about how the baby will get out, and a complex response is unnecessary.

The second principle of answering your child's questions is to be brief. If your response is direct and simple, your child will know that you feel comfortable talking about these matters and will feel free to ask you for more information when she wants it. If you overload her with too much information she will tune you out anyway.

The third principle is to use correct terms. Euphemisms confuse children. If your child is told that the baby grows in Mommy's stomach from an egg or a seed, she may believe that pregnancy and birth are part of the digestive system instead of the reproductive system!

Here are some questions you may be asked and some suggested responses. The responses are appropriate for any child old enough to ask the questions. *You may want to offer the first sentence in each response and pause to see if that is enough information to satisfy your child.*
"Where is the baby now?"

> "The baby is growing inside Mommy in a special place called her uterus. The baby is very small now, but Mommy's uterus will grow to make room for the baby to grow. You will see Mommy's belly grow bigger as the baby grows."

"How will the baby get out?"

> "When the baby is big enough to be born, Mommy will push the baby out through her vagina. Her va-

24

gina is like a tube that goes from the uterus to the outside."

"How can the baby fit into the tube?"

"Mommy's vagina will stretch so that the baby can get out. (You can show an interested child how this will happen by putting a tennis ball inside of a sock. Show your child how the tennis ball can get out of the sock by stretching the opening, and how the sock springs back to its normal size afterwards.)"

"Can daddies grow babies too?"

"No, only grown-up women can have babies because only a woman has a uterus."

"How did the baby get inside Mommy?"

"The baby grows from two tiny cells, so small that you can't even see them. The two cells are from Mommy and Daddy. The cell from Mommy is called an ovum and the cell from Daddy is called a sperm."

"How did the cell from Daddy get inside Mommy?"

"Daddy's sperm cell came from inside Daddy into Mommy through his penis. He put his penis inside Mommy's vagina and the sperm cell came out."

Remember, most young children will not ask you all of these questions. However, if they do ask you, you'll be ready and your child will learn that questions about reproduction and sex are not "off limits" in your home.

10

PREPARATION VS. OVERPREPARATION

O nce you have told your child that you are expecting a baby, you may feel that you have to follow up your announcement with discussions, books, and activities to prepare your child further.

It's helpful to remember that young children learn best when they are ready to learn and when the subject matter is interesting to them. (Actually, adults learn best under these conditions too!) If you try to get your child to learn when he doesn't want to, he'll tune you out. Some children, in fact, will walk away or even put their hands over their ears. If your child behaves this way, accept his reaction. It doesn't mean that he doesn't want you to have a baby. It only means that he's not interested in learning about the subject now.

There are three good ways to prepare your child:
- Wait for your child to ask questions or to bring up the subject of babies. If your child initiates a discussion, try to take the time to talk to him right away. Children often ask important questions just as you're rushing out the door, or trying to get them to sleep. Of course, some children also recognize that asking questions is a wonderful delaying tactic, but unless you're seeing a continuing pattern, it's a good idea to seize the moment and respond.
- Provide opportunities for your child to learn through play, stories, and casual conversation. When your child is at play you can occasionally comment on what he's doing in ways

that will help him learn about babies. If he's running around you can say, "I remember when you were a little baby and couldn't even walk!" If he's building with blocks you could say, "The baby will like watching you do that. He won't be able to play with you for a long time, but he'll like to watch."

You can also include books about babies when reading to your child. First read any books yourself before reading them to him. Some "preparation" books talk about angry or jealous feelings towards a new baby. They may be appropriate to read *after* the baby is born, but perhaps not now. If your child is not feeling this way now, she may get the idea that she *should* be!

• Include your child on some of your prenatal visits and take advantage of any special classes or tours for children at the hospital. Prenatal visits can give your child an opportunity to hear the baby's heartbeat and to meet your health care provider. Many obstetrical providers are "family centered" and will have toys and books for siblings who visit. Find out about office practices on your first prenatal visit.

Many hospitals now offer sibling preparation classes. If you have an opportunity to attend, your child will be able to learn about birth and babies in a preschool-like setting with other children (see Key 15). If your hospital doesn't offer these classes, or if your child is too young for the group activity, you can use the ideas in Keys 14, 15, and 16 to plan your own activities.

None of these preparation ideas should take up much of your time. Your child doesn't need daily or even weekly reminders of your pregnancy or the impending arrival. Occasional, informal teaching is the key to having your child prepared but not overprepared.

11

WHO GETS THE CRIB?

If your older child is still in a crib, you're probably thinking about moving her to a bed to make room for the new baby. A new bed seems like an exciting step forward for the soon-to-be big sister, and for some children it is. But other children are very attached to their cribs. There's some risk that a child who is sleeping well while enclosed in a crib will become a night wanderer when she moves into a bed. So before you rush out to purchase a new bed, consider the following:

- If you want to use the crib for the new baby right away, get your child a replacement bed a few months before the expected birth. If you want her to choose the bed herself, do some shopping ahead of time so that you can limit her choice to styles and prices that are acceptable. It's a great idea to let her pick her own sheets, even if they don't match your decorating scheme.

- After your older child has graduated to a bed, dismantle or store the old crib for a while before setting it up for the new baby. Think about buying a new set of sheets or bumper pillows so that the crib looks different and doesn't stir up too many memories for number one.

- If your older child is under two, you can leave her in her crib for now and have the new baby sleep in a bassinet or small crib until she's about five months old. It's easier to make the switch when you can talk to a child who is old enough to express herself to you in words. If you choose this option, it's still a good idea to take the crib down for a few weeks before you transfer the new baby into it.

28

- "Youth beds" aren't really necessary for a young child if you get a portable side rail for a regular bed. You don't even need the rail if you fold a blanket into a tight roll and put it under the mattress on the side away from the wall. The gentle slope will keep your child from rolling out onto the floor. But the new bed doesn't have to be a regular bed. Some children love to sleep on a mattress or futon on the floor, with a comforter or sleeping bag for warmth. The mattress can be used in a regular bed frame later when your child is past the stage of rolling out of bed.

12

IF YOU HAVE A MISCARRIAGE

No one expects to have a miscarriage, but unfortunately one in five pregnancies ends with an early fetal death, usually during the first three months of pregnancy. Any miscarriage is a painful loss to the expectant mother and father, even if there have been warning signs and symptoms such as maternal bleeding or cramping.

As parents, you may have different ways of expressing your sadness after a miscarriage. Some people cry and talk easily about their grief; others tend to hold back their feelings. Sometimes, mothers and fathers may not be able to understand what their partner is feeling, or why. The mother, who has "felt" pregnant longer, may experience a different kind of loss than the father, who has been anticipating a baby but has been less directly affected by the pregnancy thus far.

Sometimes friends and family, trying to be supportive, will respond to a miscarriage by telling parents such things as, "The baby must have had a problem anyway, and that's why you lost it," or "Don't worry, you'll get pregnant again in no time." Parents who already have one child may be told, "Well, at least you already have one child, so it's not so bad." When parents hear these kinds of responses to their loss, they may feel they are wrong or self-centered to be so sad or angry or devastated by the miscarriage. In fact, most parents do compare the loss of a pregnancy to the loss of a new baby, because, in each case, they have lost their hopes and dreams for what this new life will mean for their family. Even parents for whom the pregnancy was a surprise often feel this way. It's quite normal, and you should allow yourselves time to talk, to share your feelings, and to recover emotionally before you become pregnant again.

When you already have a child, you must also attend to his needs during your own time of sadness. A child under three will not be able to understand the concept of pregnancy, especially if he's not seen a difference in his mother's shape. He will not need an explanation about the miscarriage itself, but he will be aware that you are acting differently or seeming sad or depressed. If you have been talking about the new baby, he will notice that you have stopped such talk. It's very important to let even a young child know that you thought you would be having a baby soon, but that it turned out that you were wrong. You can tell him that you are feeling very sad, but that you will be feeling better after a while. These explanations are necessary because without them your child will feel your sadness but will not be able to understand why you are acting differently.

An older child who has been told that a baby is growing in his mother's uterus also needs to hear that the baby will not be born. Parents sometimes avoid explaining a miscarriage because it is hard to think of a way to talk about fetal death to a child in words he can understand. One way to explain your miscarriage to a child is to tell him that having a baby is sometimes like planting a garden. When we plant seeds in the spring, we hope that all of them will flower; some do, but not all. You can tell your child that the baby you were expecting was like a seed that grew into a little plant but died before becoming a flower. Tell your child how sad and disappointed you are, but also tell him that it was not his fault or anyone's fault that the baby will not be born. Young children sometimes make connections between events that adults know are not related. If your child said or thought that he was angry at you for wanting another baby, he might feel that his anger was the reason for your miscarriage.

When a miscarriage occurs, every family member needs to be there to listen, to comfort, and to respond to each other's sadness.

13

THE BIG EVENT

As you make plans for your second childbirth experience, it will be helpful to recall what labor and delivery were like for you the first time around. Although many parents have wonderful memories of the first birth, some parents can also recall moments that may have made them frightened or upset or even angry. You may have been so happy that the baby was healthy that you set aside any negative feelings about your childbirth experience. Now that you are about to give birth again, you have an opportunity to think about and talk about any disappointments from the first time, and to make realistic plans for your second time.

Realistic plans are much easier to make the second time around. No woman can really imagine the physical pain of labor until she has experienced it, and no man can imagine the difficulty of "coaching" a partner in that pain until he's had to do it. As you plan your second birth, you should talk to each other about each of your needs for support during labor.

You may also want to consider the relationship you had with your health care provider during your first pregnancy. You may have been satisfied with your care, or you may feel that you would have liked a different type of care. If your pregnancy went well, but you had a difficult childbirth experience, you may have become upset or angry with the provider you chose to help you. Sometimes you may realize that a problem in labor was not anyone's fault but still feel that your doctor or midwife should have done something differently. It's an excellent idea to talk to your provider about any of these feelings. They are not unusual for women to have, and discussing them will clear the air and strengthen your relationship. If you had such a negative experience that you have decided to change providers, you will want to discuss the first experience with your new doctor or midwife, without laying blame. A new provider can be understandably uncomfortable with a patient who is angry about a previous provider.

Keys 14–19 offer guidelines to plan for labor, delivery, birth, and the new baby during your last trimester.

14

~~~~~~

VISITING THE HOSPITAL

I f your child is more than two years old, it's a great idea to take her to visit the hospital where you will be having your baby. Hospitals can seem like scary places to a child who has never seen one. She may have heard that a hospital is a place where people go when they are sick, and she may be frightened by the idea that mommy has to go there. When a child visits, she will see that a hospital is not too different from other big buildings, and that although there are some sick people there, not everyone is ill. With some good planning on your part, she will probably even think that hospitals are interesting and fun!

Before you plan your visit, call the hospital to find out what their rules are about young children visiting, and whether there are any restrictions about hours or about areas your child can see. Some hospitals welcome children as part of the family, but others bar them from patient areas. Rules may differ among hospitals in the same community, so you may want to investigate visiting policies when you make your birth plans.

When you go to the hospital, begin by exploring the entry way and lobby. Most children will enjoy testing the automatic doors for a few moments and looking at the flowers or decorations that are usually found in hospital entrances. Wander through the lobby, looking at any interesting paintings or exhibitions. If you pass the gift shop you can take a look in but decide ahead of time whether you want to browse or shop. You don't want your visit to end in an argument over buying a toy.

After exploring the lobby, find the cafeteria. Children love the food displays usually found in hospital cafeterias, and if it is time for lunch or a snack you can stop here.

Next, if hospital rules allow, take the elevator to the maternity unit. Tell your child that because there are a lot of new mommies who need to rest it is important to speak quietly and to walk, not run, in the hallways. When you arrive at the maternity area, find the nursery where the babies are sleeping. As you and your child look through the window, she'll be able to see how small a newborn really is and, most likely, to hear how loud a newborn can cry. She'll also see the nurses caring for the babies and will have a chance to ask you questions.

Some hospitals now have special care units for premature or sick babies. If the windows for that unit are near the regular nursery, your child may wonder why those babies are so small or are attached to machines. You can tell her that some babies need special care to help them grow and get well so that they can come home and be with their families.

After you look at the babies, walk into the postpartum unit if it is allowed. As you walk by the rooms, your child will be able to see mothers, fathers, and babies and perhaps other children visiting. If you can find an empty room, let your child look inside. She'll probably be most interested in the adjustable bed, the television with the remote control, and the telephone. Let her know that the telephone is there so that mommy can call her and so that she will be able to call mommy.

As you walk around the hospital, you may see a patient pushing an intravenous (IV) bottle on a stand with a tube connected to her arm or wrist. If you do, you can point it out to your child, telling her that sometimes people have an IV to get special medicine or to help them get enough water if they can't eat or drink very much. Then, if it should turn out that a problem during childbirth makes it necessary for mom to have an IV, your child will have already seen one.

By now, you will have been walking around the hospital for at least a half hour. For a young child, that is plenty of time to take in so many new sights. Be sure to praise her for following the rules and behaving well. If she has started to get restless, you can stop your visit and return another time. You want her to think of the hospital as a nice place to visit, not a place where she got in trouble for misbehaving.

15

~~~~~~

CLASSES FOR SIBLINGS

In some communities, hospitals offer classes for young children who are expecting new babies in their families. Hospitals have found that these classes are a good way to attract parents to choose their maternity services, and to enhance their relationship with families. Sometimes, classes for children are taught by nurses from the maternity unit on Saturday mornings. They are so popular that there is usually a waiting list! This Key describes the type of class that is being taught in some hospitals.

Classes work best if the children who attend are at least three years old, since most younger children will have difficulty paying attention for long. At least one parent should accompany the child and stay throughout the class.

The class can begin with the teacher, usually a nurse from the maternity department, having the children say their names and perhaps show a picture of themselves as babies. While they are looking at the pictures, the nurse can ask them questions: "What does a baby do? What are you going to name your baby? Who is going to take care of you when your mommy comes to the hospital to have a baby?" She can display pictures or a model of a baby showing how a newborn looks, including his umbilical cord. It's often possible to show slides or have a short movie. There are many excellent educational materials that a hospital can purchase for family viewing.

The next part of the class could be a short tour of the hospital, reinforcing the positive aspects of a prior visit with mom or dad. The tour can include the details described in Key 14.

As the nurse shows the children and parents around the hospital, she can answer questions about hospital routines and give families an idea of what to expect during their stay. Children will feel comfortable about their mothers' leaving them to go to the hospital after they see for themselves where she will be and have met someone from the hospital who acts friendly and concerned.

Before the class ends, the nurse can read to the children from some selected books on babies. It's nice if the children are given certificates with their names on them proclaiming them "Official Big Brother" or "Official Big Sister." Then, while the children enjoy juice and cookies, the parents can use this opportunity to exchange names and telephone numbers for play dates or for a support group for second-time mothers.

16

~~~~~~

TEACHING OLDER CHILDREN ABOUT BABIES

I n the last months of your pregnancy you might want to teach your first child more about babies. *Always remember that the younger the child is, the more he learns by experience.* Although he can also learn through play, most real learning will take place through actual experience *after* the baby is born. If your child does not want to hear about babies now, do not worry. He may just be waiting for the real thing to arrive. In this Key you will find suggestions for teaching a child who does seem interested now.

One way to teach your child about babies is for him to observe or interact with infants at friends' homes or out in public. If you see a small newborn, ask if your child can take a peek. If you see older babies, you can explain that even though they are much bigger than your baby will be when it is born, they are still babies. One concept that is helpful to repeat to your child is that babies grow fast, but they are still babies for a long time.

Take out your child's baby pictures and tell him what he was like when he was a baby. Talk to him about how little babies cannot really do much when they are small, and about how much care they need. Remind him that in the beginning the baby will mostly sleep, feed, and cry. Tell him how you cared for him when he was a little baby, and how you plan to take good care of the new baby too, so that he will turn out as nicely as his big brother.

You may want to get your child a baby doll. Children love to play at being mothers and fathers and can learn to diaper and rock a doll while you are waiting for the real baby to arrive. After the birth, your child can then take care of "his" baby doll while you are busy with the real baby. A baby doll can also be a useful stand-in for a real baby if your child wants to act out negative feelings towards his sibling. If he gets angry and shakes his doll, you can tell him that it is all right to be angry and to be rough with a doll. If you decide to get a doll, be sure to refer to it as "your baby *doll*" not "your baby."

You can use the baby doll or a stuffed animal to show your child how to hold a baby. It's a good idea to have three rules about holding the baby that you repeat every time you practice with the doll and every time he holds the real baby:
• Always have a grownup with you when you hold the baby.
• Always sit down while you hold the baby.
• Always support the baby's head.
Show your child how to hold the baby safely. Begin by putting the doll in his lap while he is sitting down. Help him to put his left hand under the baby doll's head and his right hand under its buttocks. Always start with supporting the head.

If you are planning to bottlefeed, you can demonstrate with the doll how to hold a bottle at a tilt so that the baby doesn't swallow air. You can also show your child how to burp, diaper, and change the baby doll. Although most young children will not be able to handle helping you change a squirmy live baby, they can practice on the doll and eventually be able to help you fasten a diaper or put on a shirt.

41

Many books have been written about young children and babies, but sometimes the language level and plot are too complicated for a young child to understand. Read a book yourself before showing it to your child, to decide whether the vocabulary and concepts are at the level of other books he currently is interested in. With a little creativity, you can also make your own book. You can illustrate it yourself, or have your child draw pictures with you. You can read the book together now, and then reread it again after the baby is born. This will give you an opportunity to ask, "How is it different having a real baby from the way you thought it would be?"

17

~~~~~~

MAKING PLANS FOR LABOR AND BIRTH

E ven though you've already been through labor and delivery, it's a good idea to review what you and your husband learned in your childbirth preparation classes the first time. You probably listened very selectively then, and, like many couples, you may have assumed that you would have a "typical" or "average" labor. Now, of course, you know that there is never a typical or average labor, and that your experience, like every other mother's, was unique. However, you know more now than you knew the first time. Perhaps you felt that you could have used better relaxation techniques or that you need help in communicating your needs to the labor unit nurses. You may wish to keep your baby with you more in the hospital, or ask for more help with breastfeeding. Whatever your first experience, now is the time to reflect back upon it and make preparations for improvements.

Many parents find it helpful to take a refresher childbirth class, usually just a single session with a childbirth educator. You will be reminded of the ways you need to care for yourself during pregnancy, and encouraged to practice the breathing and relaxation techniques that can assist you in labor. If your memories of labor are unpleasant, you may want to resist thinking about labor again until you really have to. However, experienced midwives find that women who are able to recall their first births and work through the memories, especially the fear, cope much better with second-time labor.

43

If you had a Caesarean birth for your first baby, you may choose to try to have a vaginal birth for your second. The previously held belief that "once a Caesarean, always a Caesarean" is no longer considered to be true. The reason for the Caesarean the first time and the type of incision you had will determine the options for you the second time. Discuss this issue with your obstetrician and make a decision together about whether you are going to try for a VBAC (Vaginal Birth After Caesarean).

If your hospital has programs or films for expectant parents, look at the schedule and choose one or two events to attend. Even if the information is not brand new to you, you'll start to recapture a little bit of the anticipation that you felt with the first pregnancy.

Second-time pregnant women are usually relieved to know that their labor will probably progress much more rapidly than the first time. However, the more rapid labor means that you have to make plans ahead of time for getting to the hospital and for your first child's care. If you are planning to have a family member stay with you around the time of your due date, or if you live close to family or friends who can come at any time, you will feel free to leave at a moment's notice. If you don't have people nearby, or if the people you usually rely on are not available during the day, you may need to set up a schedule where different friends are "on call" for one day at a time, assuring that if you go into labor on that day someone will come to care for your young one.

You should talk to your child about what may happen if you need to go to the hospital while he is asleep or in child care. You may want to wake him for a kiss goodbye, but you should also mention the possibility that he may wake up one morning and find that Grandma or another person he knows is there. "And then you'll know you will soon be a big brother!"

18

SHOULD SIBLINGS BE
AT THE BIRTH?

As you plan the birth of your baby, you may be considering including your older child at your labor or delivery. Most parents do not choose to have a sibling present, but others do. Some parents plan a home birth in order to include a sibling, and others will choose a hospital that permits siblings to be there. Parents whose children "met" at the baby's birth often feel that there is a special closeness between the siblings that began at the shared birth experience. Although there is no way to prove that the birth experience alone determines the later relationship, it is possible that the overall experience of preparing for and sharing an important event sets a foundation for stronger relationships among all family members. However, many professionals who work with children feel that the inclusion of siblings at a birth can be psychologically damaging to the older child. The older child is exposed to a highly emotional and unpredictable event that he is not able to understand cognitively, particularly if he is under five years old.

Families who consider including siblings at birth should keep in mind that the thoughtful decision to include or not include is equally appropriate. There are potential problems as well as benefits to including children in the birth process. These guidelines will help you to decide if including your older child is right for your family.

- The older sibling should be given a choice about attending the birth. A child cannot, of course, imagine what labor and delivery will be like. Any reluctance or hesitation to attend the birth should be respected. A child should not feel pressured to be there nor should he be made to feel that it would please his parents if he attended. He should not sense that he has disappointed anyone if he expresses interest and then changes his mind.

- The older child should be accompanied throughout the labor and birth by an adult who knows him well and with whom he is very comfortable. The adult's attention should be focused primarily on the child throughout the labor and birth. Labor can last a long time, and very few children can be expected to stay interested and involved throughout. A child may become upset and need to leave if he sees his mother in pain and no one seems able to help her. The mother herself will be caught up in her own experience and cannot be expected to be available to her first child. If the child wants to leave at any time or for any reason (some children will make repeated trips to the drinking fountain), the adult must be willing to take him out immediately. Even the excitement of the birth itself can be too much for some children, and they will want to leave the room. The adult must be ready to relinquish her own desire to see the baby born if the child does not want to stay.

- The parents and child should be prepared for the birth by health care providers experienced with sibling participation at birth. In many communities there are nurses, nurse midwives, or childbirth educators who provide preparation suitable for the child's developmental level. They will meet with the parents and the child to go over plans and help the parents teach the child about birth.

- Parents should consider their child's developmental level and ability to express himself verbally before including him at the birth. A child who can talk well will be able to ask questions and get his needs met much better than a child who is not so verbally proficient. A child who is verbal but who often has difficulty in new situations may be overwhelmed by participating in such a stimulating activity. Before making any decision, think about your own child's personality.

By considering your child's needs and developmental abilities, the benefits and potential problems of including him at the birth, your family resources, and your own expectations for the birth, you can decide whether having him there is the best decision for your family.

19

BUILDING SELF-ESTEEM NOW

I f your child likes herself, she has good self-esteem. As her parents, you have both the ability and the obligation to help her to have good feelings about herself by letting her know how much you like and value her. It is important to build self-esteem both before and after the baby is born. One parent found that her efforts in making her first child feel good about himself had paid off when she said to him, soon after the new baby was born: "It must be hard when the baby takes so much attention away from you." Her son retorted: "He's NOT taking attention away from me! I'm GIVING him some of the attention!"

One of the most effective ways to build your child's self-esteem is to praise her for behavior that pleases you. Parents often take their child's good behavior for granted and only say something when the youngster misbehaves. The child then learns that she gets more attention for misbehaving. Since one of the biggest problems for an older sibling is that she gets less attention after the baby is born, it's easy to see that she might misbehave more often if she thinks that is the best way to get your attention. Teaching her now to feel proud and pleased about her good behavior will help her and you to get along better when the baby comes.

Some parents feel awkward about praising a child, but praise doesn't have to be excessive or flowery. Praise can be simple comments, such as: "I really like the way you came as soon as I called you," or, "You did a nice job of taking a bath without splashing water on the floor." In the course of a day, every child will do many things right, and it's the parents' job to notice and praise. Parents who start a pattern of consistently praising a child for things they used to take for granted often find that after a few weeks the child's good behavior increases and the misbehavior decreases. As the child's self-esteem increases she begins to want to be a more cooperative person.

Here's an example of how praise can work to help a child improve her behavior. Most first children are used to having their wants and needs met without having to wait very long. Of course, when the new baby comes, big sister *will* have to wait. If she thinks that having to wait is connected to being less important to you, she'll have a hard time. You can make it easier for her when the time comes if you start now to help her feel good about being patient.

You've probably noticed that your child will wait patiently for a time, and then get restless or fidgety or demanding. If you're like most parents, you've been waiting until that point to stop whatever you are doing and pay attention to her. However, this response can have the effect of encouraging your child to annoy you in order to get your attention!

You can help your child to wait longer and more happily by observing her while she's waiting and by watching for the *first* signs that she's getting impatient. At that point, tell her: "What a good job you're doing of waiting. I really like it when you can be so patient." Your words will reward her for what she's doing that pleases you, and will reinforce the behavior you want. At that point, finish up what you're doing as quickly as you can, and pay attention to your child. In this way, she can learn to feel good about waiting, and also discover that waiting patiently brings positive rewards.

49

The habit of noticing and praising good behavior can become a lifelong pattern in your family. Even adults may find that this technique makes them feel their efforts are appreciated. Adults often need a boost in their own self-esteem, and hearing that they've done a good job can be a bright spot in their day!

20

THE FIRST WEEKS

After your first baby was born, you may have felt as though you had just been released from a nonstop roller coaster ride, just getting through the highs and lows of labor and birth. Then, without a moment to catch your breath, you found yourself caring for a new baby who seemed to continually demand more than you thought you'd be able to give. Of course, you all survived and when you greet this next baby, you'll feel a lot more confident than you did the first time.

Even though the first few days of your new baby's life may not feel as tumultuous as when your first child was born, they still can be stressful for both the parents and the older child. You can minimize this stress to some extent by making plans for caring for yourselves during that time and by being aware of some of the common problems that may come up during the first few weeks at home.

21

THE SIBLING'S FIRST VISIT

Introducing your older child to your new baby is a special moment for the whole family. In order to make the occasion memorable, you must recognize your older child's need to feel special. Remember that she will view this big event differently than the rest of the family because, like all normal children, she sees herself as the central figure in whatever is taking place. She does not see things from your viewpoint or the baby's point of view. It's important for the adults to recognize that this is a developmentally appropriate behavior and not an indication of selfish or self-centered conduct.

Your older child will be most interested in seeing mom and making sure mom is all right. She'll want a hug and a cuddle and reassurance that she's still her mom. It will be much easier for her if when she comes into the hospital room mom is alone in bed, with arms free to hold her. If mom has had a Caesarean birth, a pillow over her abdomen will protect her and remind everyone to be gentle. After this affectionate reassurance, your child will be ready to meet the baby.

If the maternity unit has a nursery, think about having the new baby taken there right before your older child arrives. Then, after she's seen mom, it can be her job to go down with dad to the nursery to get the family's new baby. She can look in the big window and try to pick out which baby belongs to you. Her task will be much more exciting if you take a small picture of her with you when you go to the hospital. Tape the picture next to the baby's name card on the isolette, with a hand-lettered sign saying, "This is Michelle's new brother!" Your child will easily be able to find *her* new baby. After finding the baby, big sister can help roll the isolette back to mom's room. Getting a young child actively involved is always the best way to capture her interest and attention.

Back in the room, you can introduce the children in a number of ways. Dad or mom can hold the baby and unwrap him a little so that he can be seen by his sister. You can have your older child sit in a chair; then put the baby, wrapped in a blanket, in her arms for a moment. You can hold the baby in one arm and your daughter in the other and show her that you have room for both. Be sure to take a few pictures of this special time for your family album. Don't forget to show the baby's face in some of the pictures!

By now, your older child will have been visiting you for twenty to thirty minutes or longer. For many children, this is the maximum amount of time that they can be expected to be on their best behavior. Watch for clues that your child is getting bored or restless, and have dad or another family member ready to take her for a walk or back home. You don't want the first visit to end on a sour note by having to restrain your older child's activity.

Some parents like the idea of presenting the older child with a small gift "from the new baby." If your child is at the stage when he is happily appreciative of new toys, this idea may work very well for you. But if your child is at the stage when he seems to be pushing for new toys and not seeming satisfied, this may not be a good idea. Your child may view the gift as a bribe or may sense that he can now demand more toys because he's putting up with this new baby. Make your decision based on what you know about your own child's behavior with gifts.

At the end of the visit, Mom should give the older child a hug goodbye and tell him when she's coming home. She can plan to call him later in the day or in the evening. Some children will be angry and protest loudly when it's time to go. If your child cries or has a tantrum, don't be embarrassed—it's not unusual behavior for the nurses to see. Give your child an extra hug and let him leave quickly. However, don't be surprised if he acts casual or uninterested about leaving his mother behind. Children all differ in the ways that they handle separation, and some children may act as though it's no big deal that Mom is out of the house for a while, even though they miss her very much. A second-time mother may even feel as though she's suddenly lost the affection of her first child. Be assured, this is just your child's way of coping with change.

22

BRINGING BABY HOME

In many community hospitals mothers are discharged with their new babies one day after the birth. Many insurance policies will pay only for the overnight stay unless the mother or baby has a complication. If you anticipate this short a stay in the hospital, you will want to plan for the extra help and support that you will need at home to care for both you and the baby. Even with help, these transition days can be difficult as you begin to care for two children instead of one.

If your older child comes in the car to bring the baby home, you can show her how you'll keep the baby safe by using an infant car seat. This is a good time to start telling your child about all the things you used to do for her when she was a little baby, and how you'll be caring for the new infant in the same way. At the same time, your child will see that she is old enough to use a "big girl's" car seat (or if she is older than four years old and weighs more than forty pounds, a passenger seat belt).

Some families like to have a little welcome home party for the new baby, with a small cake bought or made ahead of time and stored in the freezer. This can be a festive occasion that lets your older child participate in a way that is fun and special for her, since she will be the only child old enough to eat the cake! The welcome home party can also include an exchange of gifts. If the older child wants to, she can choose or make a present to give to the new baby. One gift that many older children enjoy receiving is a T-shirt that says "I'm the Big Sister" or "I'm the Big Brother."

Even if your child has already met the baby in the hospital, the excitement of the first visit there and the distractions of the unfamiliar hospital environment may have interfered with her remembering very much. The younger a child is, the more times you will have to show her and tell her all the rules and reminders about caring for a new baby. Since her continued interest will be in how the new baby affects *her*, she may pay only brief attention to him now and seem uninterested. Or she may find him as fascinating as a new toy, and your task will be setting limits on her behavior. Either way, think of your homecoming as being the first step in the journey towards helping your older child to accept, care for, and love her younger sibling.

If you will have relatives or friends at home to help you in the first few days, be sure you talk to them about making your older child feel included. Sometimes a well-intentioned adult can upset a child by telling her that she is naughty for disturbing her mother's sleep, or that she can't go into her mother's room while she's feeding the baby. Everyone in the family needs to remember to pay attention to the older child in a positive way.

One concern that parents may have is how to prevent the new baby from catching a cold or other illness from family members, including the sibling, or from visitors. It's wise to keep away anyone with an infection, but since most young children are often just coming down with or just getting over a cold, it's not realistic to think that you can totally protect the new baby. The most valuable protection is to have everyone wash hands before touching the baby. If all the adults follow this rule, it will not be difficult to have your child wash her hands as well. Another way of protecting the new baby is to allow only your own child to hold him in the first few weeks or months. Allowing other children to touch him or hold him only increases the chance of infection. Also, if your child is the only one who has the privilege and responsibility of holding her new baby, she will feel special and even more protective towards him.

As you settle the baby into your home, explain to your older child what you are doing and why. For example, if the baby is going to sleep in a cradle, you can explain that little babies like to feel cozy in small spaces and that the blankets help to keep him warm. If the cradle is in your room, you can point out that you need to have the baby close by at first because you will have to hear him to feed him during the night. If you give the baby a pacifier, you can tell your child that new babies like to suck even when they aren't hungry. Children love to learn about new things that they can see, and, for some children, a new baby is like a wonderful new doll that is real.

You can also begin showing your older child some of the baby's reflexes that will probably capture her interest. A new baby will grasp a finger and hold on tight, and your older child will probably love to feel his tiny hand touching hers. When the baby startles at a sudden movement or loud noise, explain that you have to be gentle and quiet with a new baby, because he is not able to handle much noise or excitement.

Your child may be bothered by the way the cut umbilical cord looks and will ask for an explanation. You can tell her that when the baby was in your uterus he couldn't eat or drink, and that the cord was connected to you. He received all of his nourishment through the connecting cord.

When the baby was born, the cord was cut, because now the baby can drink milk. Your child may want to know if it hurt the baby to have the cord cut. You can tell her that there are no nerves for feeling in the cord, touching her arm to demonstrate "feeling," and that it didn't hurt the baby at all. Tell her that the dark, dry cord will fall off soon, leaving his navel to look like his big sister's, who was born in just the same way.

If your new baby was circumcised, your older child may notice the reddened tip of his penis and ask what happened. It is usually best to give a very simple explanation, telling the child that the doctor cut a small piece of skin at the end of the baby's penis and that the redness she sees will soon go away. If circumcision is part of your religious tradition, you can explain that it is a part of being Jewish or Islamic that baby boys are circumcised. If your older child is a boy, you can tell him that he was circumcised too, and that his penis and the baby's penis will look the same.

Many children will ask lots of questions and want to be very involved in finding out about the new baby. Other children will almost ignore the new arrival. Most children will fall somewhere in between the two extremes. As you get through the first few days, be prepared to accept your child's behavior for the moment and to allow him to work through his reactions at his own pace.

23

~~~~~~

POSTPARTUM RECOVERY: THE SECOND TIME

After your first baby was born, you were probably told to expect some emotional ups and downs in addition to the physical symptoms that are part of a woman's hormonal and psychological responses to giving birth. With your second birth, you may have forgotten these normal responses, and you and your older child may not be prepared for this aspect of childbirth.

If you remember experiencing these highs and lows as well as some physical discomforts after your first child was born, it will be easier to plan for them the second time. Of course, many women don't remember, just as their memories of their first labor and birth dim over time!

Some women feel exhilarated right after giving birth. This feeling can sometimes persist for days and make you feel as though you have the energy to do everything: take care of your baby, your older child, your house, and even guests. It's easy to become overloaded and exhausted, because you genuinely feel great. Unfortunately, the "high" is almost always followed by a "low," and if you don't moderate your activities, you may find yourself crying with weariness and despair when the visitors you invited finally do go home.

It's helpful if husbands can protect you during this somewhat labile period. It's important for dads to take over routine chores and give you time alone each day to bathe, nap, or just pamper yourself for a little bit. At times, Dad may need to protect your older child from being confused or upset by your mood swings. If you are crying or feeling overwhelmed, it's very important to tell your child that it's not because of anything he's done. Let him know that you are a little tired or cranky because you've just had a baby, but that as you get stronger you'll feel better.

Some women may find that the sad and dreary feelings that sometimes follow childbirth do not get better, or may even become worse. If you continuously feel sad, and if taking care of yourself and your children is becoming more difficult, you may be experiencing postpartum depression. This is a treatable condition, and you should consult with your obstetrician or health care provider.

Physical discomforts are not unusual postpartum and can be more stressful the second time because the mother cannot rest as much. One serious problem often overlooked is *anemia* (not enough red blood cells). This frequently occurs because of blood loss and metabolic alterations at the time of birth. It's very important to continue to take your prenatal vitamins and iron until your six-week checkup. If you are feeling tired, weary, or mildly depressed at that time, ask to have your blood level checked, since anemia can cause these symptoms.

Another common source of discomfort for second-time mothers is *after pains*, the cramping abdominal pains caused by the uterus contracting as it returns to its original size. These contractions are often unnoticed following a first birth, but can be quite severe after your second birth because your uterus has been stretched more and is not as resilient as it was the first time. The after pains are more likely to be felt during breastfeeding because the same hormones that cause your breasts to release milk cause your uterus to contract. Many women find that the pain is more manageable if they take acetaminophen before nursing.

The most common physical discomfort after a second pregnancy is *fatigue.* In fact, second-time mothers, unlike first-time mothers, usually report that the fatigue they feel is much more stressful than any of the discomforts of pregnancy or even the pain of childbirth itself. The fatigue is, of course, largely due to lack of sleep. With a new baby, it is inevitable that nighttime sleep will be interrupted every three to four hours in order to nurse or bottle feed. But the responsibilities of caring for an older child can make it impossible for the postpartum mother to nap or even rest during the day to make up for the nighttime sleep deprivation. It's very important for husbands, family, and friends to try to help the mother find time every day to sleep or at least relax. If possible, both the older child and the baby can be taken for a walk or a ride. While the baby naps in the afternoon, the older child can visit a friend or watch a favorite TV show or video for an hour to let Mom rest. It's ideal if the baby and the older child can nap at the same time, but such a schedule is often a happy coincidence rather than a scheduled plan.

If the new mother of two feels overwhelmed by household responsibilities, she may take avantage of the children's naps to try to get housework or deskwork accomplished. Asking friends to help by shopping, running errands, or preparing meals is a great way to save your strength (some women request home-cooked meals as a baby shower present!).

If Mom is continuing an out-of-home career, she may be on the telephone in spare moments handling unfinished details of work interrupted by the birth. Co-workers, especially those without children or those who have not been responsible for a new baby in a long time, may not be sensitive to her need to recover.

A "super mom" juggling act can add to the stress and fatigue of the first weeks and result sometimes in illness. It is not wise to push your body or your emotional resources during the postpartum period. Caring for yourself now will result in more energy and good health in the months to come.

24

BREASTFEEDING THE BABY WHEN YOU HAVE AN OLDER CHILD

If you breastfed your older child and enjoyed it, you are probably planning to breastfeed your new baby. At the same time, you may be wondering how you will find the time to nurse the baby while your older child is demanding your attention. You probably remember the frequent feedings your first baby needed, and the many times you had to stop what you were doing to respond to a hungry baby's cry. How will you be able to do the same thing now with an older child needing you too?

Most mothers find that nursing the second baby *is* often a bit of a juggling act, but they also find that the convenience of nursing far outweighs the difficulties. It's very easy to nurse the baby while you are talking, reading, or even playing with your older child. You don't have to stop to prepare or warm a bottle when the baby cries, and many breastfed babies are content to suck at the breast for comfort long after they are full, allowing you some peaceful moments.

Older children will have some reactions and often some jealousy as they watch you nurse their new sibling. It's very helpful if you can show the big sister some baby pictures taken when she was nursing. Even if you don't have pictures, talk to her about how healthy the baby will be, just like her, because she nurses. You can also tell her that the baby will need to nurse often because she's growing so fast.

As your child watches you nurse, she may want to be held and cuddled the way she sees you cuddling the baby. Try nursing in bed or on a sofa where there is enough room to have one of your children on each side of you.

It's not unusual for the older child to want to try nursing again too. Although the idea may seem rather startling to you and perhaps even distasteful, this desire really is no different from all the other "playing baby" types of demands you can expect from her during this adjustment time (see Key 28). You can express a little milk into a teaspoon and let her try it. Most children will be surprised by the taste of breast milk. They are used to cold, fresh cow's milk. Your milk will be body temperature, thin, and rather sweet tasting. For most children, their interest will end there. However, if your child does still want to try nursing, you should let your own feelings on the matter be your guide. If the idea of letting her nurse at your breast puts you off, just tell her firmly, "No, breast-feeding is for babies only." If you don't mind her trying, hold her and let her put her mouth to your nipple. She probably won't be able to nurse, because the movement of a nursing baby's jaws and tongue is not easy for an older child to co-ordinate. Let her try, and then tell her that she can cuddle with you but that her nursing time is over. Most children's curiosity will be satisfied at that point, and that will be the end of the matter.

A far more common problem when you are breastfeeding a second baby is amusing the older child while you are trying to sit quietly and nurse. If your child is under three, you will probably want her close by at all times, unless your home is so thoroughly childproofed that you can trust her out of your sight. Some parents will have a special basket of toys that comes out only during nursing times. You can rotate toys through the basket so that there is often a surprise. Some of the toys can be simple puzzles or games that you can do with one hand. Many mothers and children find that the nursing time is a wonderful time to read. You can keep a supply of picture books near all of the spots where you usually sit to nurse.

The slightly older child may be able to play by herself or even watch a video or TV program while you nurse. However, older children, although they may be generally safe playing out of your sight, are also smart enough to realize that they can easily interrupt you by getting into trouble in another room. If you find that you have a child who always seems to be calling for help while you're nursing, it's a good idea to have her stay in the room with you. Young children don't have enough impulse control to walk the line between crying "wolf" and actually endangering themselves.

Some mothers worry that the new baby is missing out on the intimacy of the breastfeeding experience because mom is also paying attention to the older child. In fact, some second-time mothers say that they enjoy the middle-of-the-night feedings because it is the only time they feel they can be alone with the baby without being distracted! Fortunately, a new baby can't really tell if his breastfeeding mother is giving him her full attention. One of the wonderful advantages of breastfeeding is that as the baby snuggles warmly in her arms, he is feeling the mother's smooth skin, hearing her heartbeat, and satisfying his hunger with her warm milk. He is enveloped in a nurturing environment, even if Mom is reading to big sister at the same time.

If you are breastfeeding, remember that fatigue can affect your milk supply. Even if you can't nap regularly, don't take on any more activities than you have to. If your baby is not gaining weight or if you are having breastfeeding difficulties, ask yourself if you are getting too busy. It takes energy to make breast milk, so take care of yourself by resting, eating a well-balanced diet, and continuing to take your prenatal vitamins and iron.

25

BOTTLEFEEDING THE
BABY WHEN YOU HAVE
AN OLDER CHILD

If parents choose to bottlefeed their new baby, the mother will be able to share the responsibility of feeding the little one. Some mothers choose to combine breast- and bottlefeeding for this reason, using either expressed breast milk or infant formula in the bottles. Other mothers prefer to bottlefeed only.

If you decide to use a baby bottle, your older child will in all likelihood want one for himself. This is very appropriate behavior from a young child's point of view. After all, the baby seems to be enjoying the bottle, so why shouldn't her sibling enjoy it also? Many children find sucking to be very soothing and comforting in times of stress, and the changes occurring around the time a new baby is born are certainly very stressful.

Most parents feel comfortable allowing the older child to take a bottle at least some of the time, setting limits depending on his age and stage of development. If your child is under three, he might have a bottle while you are feeding the baby and while he is going to sleep. An older child who requests it should be given the bottle and also told, "It's nice to pretend that you're a baby too, isn't it?" Whatever limits you choose to set, be sure to do so without criticizing the older child. If you get into a battle over this symbol of babyhood, you will make the issue even more important. Don't forget to tell other adults that it is all right with you that he is using the bottle for now and that you don't want anyone to make fun of him or tell him that he shouldn't act like a baby (see Key 28).

If you do allow your older child to have a bottle, it's important for his health that the liquid in the bottle be water only, because milk or juice in a bottle will coat the back of his teeth as he sucks. This coating may eventually break down the enamel on his teeth and cause decay. This kind of decay is very difficult and painful to treat, so it is important to protect your child. If your older child is already attached to a milk or juice bottle, you can wean him by gradually adding water to the bottle. Begin by adding one ounce of water to each bottle to replace the other liquid. Add one more ounce every other day, and at the end of two weeks your child either will be taking water only or will have stopped using the bottle.

Your older child may also want to help you feed the baby with a bottle. It's not advisable to allow him to do this on his own, since he may not be able to hold the baby and the bottle carefully enough to prevent choking. You can allow him to sit with you while you feed the baby, and you can give him a bottle to feed to a baby doll or a stuffed animal. Keep in mind that his offers to help may also be pleas for attention. He may just want to be included while you are feeding the baby. Have him sit near you and read to him or tell him a story while you are feeding the baby.

When you are bottlefeeding a baby and your older child needs you, or other responsibilities distract you, it can be very tempting to prop the baby's bottle for a moment. However, a baby can accidentally choke or regurgitate milk into her lungs when her bottle is propped, even if you do so for just a moment. In addition, your baby will be being deprived

68

of your love and attention while she is satisfying her hunger. So be sure to cuddle the baby close to you while you feed her, so that she can feel your body's warmth, hear your heartbeat, and gaze at your face. That's how she learns that the world is a place where she can always count on someone to nurture and love her.

26

~~~~~~

WHAT TO EXPECT

The first three months caring for your new baby and expanded family will be unpredictable. Your life will be determined, in many ways, by the needs of your baby. If your baby is calm, predictable, and easy to care for, you may begin to feel that raising two children seems easier than you ever could have imagined. On the other hand, if your baby is "high need" and demands a lot of rocking, soothing, and feeding, and very little sleep, you might find yourself wondering how *anyone* can manage more than one child. Most likely, you will find that your baby is somewhere in between the two extremes and that your responses will be that way as well.

Other factors besides the baby can contribute to how your first three months go. You may have other demands on your time from family members, friends, or work. Even a minor illness in your older child (especially if she passes it on to you and the new baby) can upset even the best-laid plans.

Your older child's response to the new baby will be hard to predict, no matter how she has behaved during your pregnancy and how much preparation you have done. Children are different in the way they adjust to change, and just as the baby's level of need will affect your response, it may also affect your child's response.

In Keys 27 through 30 you will find ideas for minimizing your child's negative reactions to the new baby. You will also read about some common adjustment reactions to the birth

70

of a sibling, and some ideas for coping with them. Keep in mind that some children do not react to a new baby at first. Your older child may not feel, in the first three months, as though her life has been disrupted at all. You may not see any of the responses described in these Keys for now, but they may emerge later as the baby becomes a more active member of the household. Keep this information in mind as you deal with problems that might come up six months, or even a year, from now.

27

GIVING ATTENTION TO NUMBER ONE

No matter how much you enjoy spending time with your older child, you will find that your time together is more limited than it was before the new baby arrived. More importantly, even if you give your child what seems to be as much attention as you possibly can, the distraction of the new baby may make her feel as though she's never getting enough of your time. Try to remember that young children live in the moment. Even if you took the afternoon off on Monday to go to the zoo, your child won't care on Thursday morning when she wants you and you're too busy to play.

Since you can't carve out more than twenty-four hours from a day, and since there are many demands on your time that cannot be set aside, you will have to figure out how to give attention to your older child so that she will feel less deprived. The best way is to spend a short time with her *every* day, calling it "special time." This time is not a substitute for your usual interactions with her. It is a bonus, to make your child feel special when she may not be feeling special at all.

Special time lets your child know that you care about her, that you are interested in her, and that you want to be with her, even if you are often busy. Special time is a way to keep your child feeling secure and to avoid the buildup of tension that can lead to tantrums or deliberate misbehavior.

To plan for special time, choose a period during the day that you realistically can expect to spend with her *every* day without any distractions. For most parents, this will be about fifteen to twenty minutes. It's helpful to use a timer to mark the time. During this time, have someone else care for the baby unless you're sure he'll be asleep. Don't answer the telephone, and ask your family and friends not to interrupt you.

Tell your child that even though you are very busy with the baby and other things, you want to make sure that the two of you have time together every day that is special. Let her choose the activity: this point is important. Often parents select the activity that *they* want, and the child soon realizes that the only way she can get attention is by going along with the parents' idea of fun! Don't be surprised if your child wants you to play with her by *watching* her play, or by being a character in a drama she invents. She may want to be in her room or go outdoors. The only restrictions that you should make are if she chooses an activity that is unsafe or cannot be done in the time you have.

At the end of special time, tell your child that time is up for the day but that you will have special time again the next day. If your child wants to play longer by herself, she can, but you should end your part. You can play with her again later, but you want her to know that special time is the same every day. For a young child, this kind of ritual is very satisfying, and eventually you will find that saying, "Not now, but we can do that in our special time," will satisfy her.

If you are really too busy to give your child special time every day, try for every other day, or even three times a week. If even that much time is too hard, it's a good idea to look at whether you've taken on too many other responsibilities.

28

REGRESSION

The most common way that an older child will respond to the birth of a sibling is by *regression*. Regression means, very simply, going backwards. You should not be at all surprised if your older child at some point begins to act the way he did when he was younger.

For some children, the step backward will be to lose some of the skills they have most recently acquired. For example, the child who has been out of diapers for several months will frequently begin to have accidents. The child who has been dressing herself will suddenly be unable to do so without help. The child who has been falling asleep easily at night will want an extra story or a drink of water or will want someone to lie down with him. As a parent, you may be torn between feeling sympathy for your child and frustration at his not being able to do what you know he could do in the past. If the areas of his regression create more work for you, your frustration will of course be greater.

Other children demonstrate regression by taking what seems to be a giant step backwards: they start to act like babies. Your child might begin talking baby talk, or wanting a bottle, or needing to carry around a comfort item. For many parents, this babylike behavior is very upsetting. You may feel that caring for one new baby is work enough, and that a second "baby" is way too much. It can be very tempting to tell an older child to "Stop acting like a baby. You're too old to act that way!"

A look at some causes of regression in young children can help you decide how to respond most effectively. First, regression is a very common response for anyone undergoing stress. Most people, in times of stress, turn to the familiar for comfort. An adult who is upset might want a glass of warm milk or a remembered childhood food, or might even long to crawl into bed and pull the covers up over her head! If adults can feel this way, it's not surprising that a child under stress would want to behave in a way that is more childish for *him*.

The second reason for children to regress following the arrival of the new baby is that they are reacting to seeing you give attention to all the babylike behaviors that they have given up. A young child typically makes connections of cause and effect based on what he sees. "The baby wears diapers, cries, sucks on a pacifier, and gets a lot of attention. If I act the way the baby does, then I will get more attention, too."

The best way for parents to respond to any kind of regression on the part of an older child is to accept his need to act out his feelings, but at the same time help him to see that acting his age is a better way to get attention. For example, you can say to a child who is toilet trained but has had an accident, "Oh, I guess you forgot that you're not wearing diapers." Even if the accidents persist, act matter-of-fact and refrain from showing anger or annoyance. If he was only recently trained, you might decide to put him back in diapers for a few weeks, but if he's been in pants for a while and is having only one or two accidents a day, it is better to continue considering him "trained." The same advice applies to other regressive behaviors. Tolerate them matter-of-factly, and assume that they are just a phase your child needs to go through as he adjusts to his new sibling.

The other approach that you should take to your child's regression is to point out to him the things you see him doing that are "grown-up." For example, when the baby cries, you can say to him, "I'm so glad that you are three years old and that you can tell me what you need instead of having to cry." You can also share with your child that you get tired sometimes of the work and attention the baby needs. You can tell your child that you will be glad when the baby is old enough to dress herself, or no longer needs diapers, and can fall asleep without crying. Gradually, your older child will realize that even though the baby gets attention for her babyish behavior, he can still get positive attention for his "big boy" behavior.

Remember that, from a child's point of view, his parents can never give him enough time. If he is being asked to share that time with someone else, he will quite reasonably be trying to do things that he believes will get it back. By following the guidelines in this Key and in Key 27, you will be able to minimize, although not eliminate, his need to regress.

29

ANGER, JEALOUSY, AND AGGRESSION

Most parents realize that there will be times when their older child will feel anger or jealousy about the new baby, and that these feelings may be expressed by aggressive behavior. It is reasonable to have this expectation because anger and jealousy are universal emotions among all ages of people. When children are angry or jealous, they may express these feelings by hitting, fighting, or being verbally provocative. It is important that you not feel that the birth of a sibling is the root of any problems you might have with your child in these areas. You would be dealing with these issues whether or not you have another child. As a parent, you cannot protect your child from having to manage unpleasant feelings. In fact, it is your job as a parent to help him learn that it is possible to feel bad, but to behave appropriately. In this Key, you will learn how to respond to anger, jealousy, and aggression in your child, regardless of the cause.

When a young child feels bad, he often acts on his feelings in a childlike, or childish, way. He may cry, or have a tantrum, or yell, or throw something. He may hit or pinch. Such behavior helps him to discharge the tension that results from his bad feelings. Of course, the problem with acting this way is that his action tends to provoke a response from others that increases the tension. Often he will find that when he expresses his feelings loudly or aggressively, the adults around him react by also being loud and aggressive. The result is an explosion of bad feelings, and both child and parents end up feeling frustrated and exhausted when the battle is over. If the pattern of anger and aggression continues, parents and child will soon be trapped in a cycle of blowups followed by brief truces that last only until the next blowup.

When your child acts angry, in words or actions, you can help him best if you teach him to express himself *in words* that communicate how he feels. For example, a child who is playing with a toy may not want to be interrupted to get ready for bed. He may resist and say "No, go away, I hate you," while at the same time he hits you. It is better for your child if, hard as it might be, you can stay calm, ignore the words and actions, and instead respond to what you know he is *feeling.* "You want to keep playing and it is time for bed. You're angry at me for making you go to bed." Although it may be difficult to react calmly to a child who is out of control, this is the only response that will work to teach your child that yelling or hitting is not an appropriate way to express anger. If you lose control, your child will never learn how to control himself.

If you can teach your child, over time, that it is all right to say, "I'm *MAD!*" but that it is not all right to throw a toy or hit you, he will be learning to express his feelings in a constructive way. Children need to learn that it is better to express angry feelings verbally rather than physically. As they get older, they can learn "nicer" ways of letting others know they are angry.

Some parents get very upset when their child expresses anger, especially if the anger is directed towards them. "How can my child talk to me this way?" they think. Parents may get so upset with the child that he will be afraid to direct his anger towards them. However, if the child is not taught more positive ways to express himself, he will simply direct his anger towards others. The child who hits other children may be acting this way because his parents do not allow him to express his anger in an appropriate way towards them. This misdirection of anger occurs quite commonly after parents have brought a new baby into the family.

The following story illustrates the impact of a new baby on an older child. Imagine a happily married woman whose husband comes home one day and announces, "Guess what, honey. I've decided to have another wife! She'll be joining us soon. I've enjoyed having you as a wife so much that I know I'll be even happier if I have another wife just as wonderful as you are—in her own way, of course. And then you'll have another wife to keep you company! Won't that be great?" How do you think that wife would react? She would probably be pretty angry at her husband for thinking that she should welcome someone into her life to compete for his time and attention. This story illustrates why it is more appropriate for children to become angry with their *parents* for having a new baby, rather than to take out the anger on the baby himself.

This doesn't mean that at times your child might *not* get mad at the new baby. But if your child is angry with you and you won't let him express himself, even in words, it is quite likely that he will vent his feelings on his sibling. Encouraging your child to let you know how he is feeling while you are being accepting and understanding of his feelings, is important.

When your child acts cranky or difficult, you can say to him, "I wonder if you are feeling left out when I'm holding the baby so much," or "It must be hard to have to wait while I'm busy with the baby. It can make you feel angry." You can also tell your child that it is all right to act out his feelings in a way that doesn't hurt anyone. If your child has a baby doll or stuffed animal, you can encourage him to say to the doll what he'd like to say to you or the baby: "Put that baby down and play with me!" or "Stop crying, you stupid baby!"

Some children will want to hit or throw the doll. You can say to your child, "When you get mad and want to hit or throw something, it's O.K. to hit a doll. You can't hurt a doll." But if your child wants to hit you or the baby, you should stop him right away and say, "No. I will not let you hit me. I won't let you hurt someone else, and I also won't let someone else hurt you."

Some of the words suggested in this Key may sound artificial to you. By all means, substitute your own, but pay attention to the *way* you talk to your child when he is out of control. By choosing your words carefully, you will demonstrate to your child that his anger is not frightening to you, and that you can respond to him calmly no matter how upset he is. Over time, he will learn that he, too, can manage his emotions.

30

SHARING A ROOM

D o siblings need separate rooms? Are there problems when two children share a room? There was a time when these questions would have seemed silly to ask. Most families, then, took it for granted that children would share a room, and the idea of separate bedrooms was unheard of. However, as more and more single-family homes were built in the late 1950s and early 60s, families began to look for homes with as many bedrooms as they could afford. It eventually became common—and desirable—for families with two or three children to have enough bedrooms for the parents and each child as well.

We are now in a new era of housing availability in this country. Many families live in city apartments and in areas where the price of housing has dramatically increased. For these families, it may be difficult or impossible to find affordable housing with enough bedrooms for the parents and each child. Parents who were raised with the idea that children do not share bedrooms may worry that there will be problems if their own children must share. Usually, these worries are unfounded.

If you would like your children to share a room, you should be matter-of-fact about your plans. Don't give your older child the idea that the choice to share is one that she can make. As you begin talking about the baby coming, you can tell her that the baby will be sharing her room, and that it will now be the "children's room." As you begin setting up for the baby, add any furniture that will be needed. If you need to rearrange the existing furniture, ask your older child to help. She may have some good ideas about how to fit things in, or at this point she may want to express her desire that the baby not move in. If she seems resistant, it's important to acknowledge her feelings but to continue to be matter-of-fact: "You wish the baby didn't have to share your room. You'd like to keep having the room to yourself. But this is where the baby will be sleeping."

Some parents worry that the new baby will wake up the older child during the first few months. If your older child is a light sleeper, you might want to keep a cradle or bassinet or portable crib in your room for the baby to sleep in at first. Set up the space in your older child's room anyway, so that the baby can at least take naps there. It's not unusual for an older child to start looking forward to the time when the baby is old enough to sleep in the "children's room" with her.

Another concern that parents may have is room sharing by opposite-sex children. Eventually, brothers and sisters will need—and want—to sleep separately, but that time will come after the preschool years. A four-year-old may want to have privacy from little sister or brother, but this can be accomplished by providing separate times for bathing, and rules for *not* watching during dressing. The children can have privacy without having separate rooms. Privacy can also be an issue if the children have toys or collections that they do not wish to share. You eventually may want to create some dividers in the room that can mark off personal space.

Separate bedrooms really are not necessary for the healthy growth and development of your children. Most children who share bedrooms have positive feelings about the sharing. If siblings argue about their room, they probably would be arguing about something else if the room were not the issue. If you do all that you can to promote a good sibling relationship, where the children sleep will not be a problem.

31

RESTRUCTURING FAMILY LIFE

The first three months of life with your second baby may be busy, exhausting, or even overwhelming as you add the tasks of new-baby care to the work of your preexisting family. But most parents say that, despite the additional physical demands, the new baby doesn't seem to demand much of their emotional energy until he starts to interact with other family members. Most babies start to "wake up" when they're around three months old. They begin to stretch their wakeful alert time from minutes to hours. The newborn baby who may have cried only when he was hungry, sleepy, or wet may now begin to fuss when he is bored. He's learned to smile and laugh and respond to the people around him, and his reactions engage further responses from them. He is entertaining and wants to be entertained himself.

First time around, you probably were delighted by this wonderful time in your baby's life. Every day was new and exciting as your baby became what many parents describe as "a real person." Second-time around can be equally exciting, especially as you notice the different ways the new baby responds to you and the world. Parents often say that they hadn't realized how unique each child in their family was until they saw how different the second child was from the first.

However, these differences also add to the complexity of caring for two children. What worked for your first child doesn't always work for your second. The second child will evoke different responses from each parent, and both children will act differently when they are either alone with one parent, or in the presence of both parents. Family interactions not only will seem to be, but actually *will* be, much more complicated. Diagrams of your new family structure may help demonstrate this point.

When you are a couple without children, you are able to communicate directly with one another. One person speaks or gestures, the other person listens or watches and responds. The two-way communication pattern can be illustrated like this:

Mom ●⇌⎯⎯⎯⎯⎯⎯⎯⎯⎯→● Dad

As simple as this two-way communication pattern looks, couples know that there are times when one person misunderstands the other because the speaker does not express himself clearly, or the listener hears incorrectly, or the message has a different meaning for each participant. Communication then becomes miscommunication.

After your first child is born, the family communication pattern looks like this:

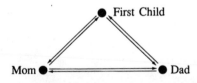

Instead of two communication pathways, you now have six. Each person has different ways of letting the other know what he wants to say. When more people are involved in a conversation, you have less time to see if what is said is understood the way it is meant. Once you become parents, you may feel that you aren't communicating as well as you used to, and these pathways illustrate one reason why. (For more about the couple relationship, see Key 36.) With two children added to the family, there are now four of you, and here is the diagram of your communication pathways:

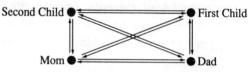

There are twelve different paths of communication in your family, with twice as many opportunities for miscommunication as you had just a few months ago! So if family life is starting to feel complicated, the ideas and suggestions in Keys 32 through 36 will give you some tools for coping with this complexity.

32

JUGGLING THE WORK OF TWO

When you have only one child, it's fairly easy to be flexible. With two parents available, you can take turns meeting the youngster's needs and still have a little time for yourselves. You may have found that you enjoyed being able to take your first child many places, without having to worry too much about what time he went to sleep or when he ate. If your firstborn was a fairly adaptable child, you may not have felt that you needed to follow much of a schedule or routine.

With two children, you probably will find that family life works better if you develop routines and structure. There are two reasons to do this. First, your older child, as he starts to get a sense of the pattern of each day, will be able to regulate himself more and more if he knows what to expect. Two- and three-year-old children are testing limits all the time. The best way for you to help your child achieve some self-control is to keep the limits as consistent as possible. For example, it is normal for a two-and-a-half-year-old to resist bedtime. Therefore, if your child knows that bedtime is flexible and that the bedtime routine varies from night to night, he will struggle with you every evening to prolong the routine and to stay awake as late as possible. If he knows that bedtime is fixed and that he only gets a set amount of stories and drinks of water, he will go to sleep with much less fuss.

The second reason to develop routines and structure is that, with two children at different ages and with different needs, you will need a schedule or you will be overwhelmed by their demands. Your baby's schedule, of course, will have to conform to her changing needs for feeding and sleep. Your older child's schedule will reflect his "inner clock" as well, but he can be expected to adapt more readily to a family routine because he is more mature. Having a predictable routine and planning how you will divide responsibilities for your children's care will make it possible for you to get through your days without altogether losing control of your time.

Some parents resist the idea of a schedule or set routines because they feel that their child is too unpredictable to be able to conform. It is true that some children (and adults) are temperamentally more irregular than others. However, a child who doesn't have a built-in rhythm is often happier if his parents gently impose a structure to his life.

If you have a child who has an irregular and unpredictable appetite, for example, you may be in the habit of feeding him any time he seems hungry, rather than at regular times. Although his nutritional needs will be met by this approach, you will feel like a short-order cook before very long. You can create a structure that will work for all of you by offering him a small meal or snack every two hours throughout the day, whether he seems hungry or not. Let him choose whether to eat or not. If you continue to offer food without waiting for him to demand it and if you match some of his meals with yours or the baby's feeding times, your child will begin to learn about eating and waiting for meals. In the next Key you'll find ideas for building other routines into your daily lives.

33

GETTING ON A SCHEDULE

M any parents resist a schedule for themselves because they feel that their lives away from home are so busy that they want to be able to relax when they're with their families. This feeling is quite understandable from an adult's point of view, but the fact is that most children find routines helpful. Children, as a rule, seem more relaxed when they know what to expect. If you observe a well-run nursery school program, you will notice that there are many predictable events throughout the morning. If you ask a three-year-old what she does each day, you'll hear a more self-confident tone from the child who *knows* what happens each day than from the child whose day unfolds differently, depending on the mood of her parents.

Every family has a different schedule that works for them. Here are some routines that work well particularly for families with a young child and a new baby.

Have a morning routine for the older child that includes cuddling or some special time, even if it's just for a few minutes. Many children like to climb into bed with their parents for a hug. During this time you can talk to your child about the day—what he's going to do, where he'll be, what the weather will be like, and whether you have planned any special activities. This time is important, because if you don't give your child positive attention in the morning, he's sure to

89

demand negative attention by resisting you or arguing with you when you're trying to get him going.

Have a sequence of events for feeding the children and getting dressed. Some parents find that it works well for each parent to handle one child. In other families, one parent gets dressed while the other cares for the children. In some families, one parent does everything while the other sleeps late! This last approach works well if the mother is still waking up to feed the baby during the night. Dad can manage both children while mom gets a little extra rest to carry her through the day. The most important part of the morning routine is to have a general understanding of who does what and when. It's hard on everyone, but particularly on your older child, if the morning is disorganized or tense because the plans are unclear.

Once the family is dressed, your day will unfold. Plan activities that allow you to have the children nap or rest at about the same time every day. If your older child is in a nursery school or day care program, make sure that he knows what your plans will be when you pick him up. Schedule your afternoon and evening routines to include relaxed time to play with him, even if it's just for a few minutes while the baby is asleep.

The evening routine will probably include dinner, bath, and bedtime activities. Most young children will eat better if dinner is served early. If you want your child to sit with you for a later meal, offer him a snack between five and six o'clock, and keep your expectations low for his behavior and appetite at the main meal. Many children enjoy watching children's programs such as "Mister Rogers" or "Sesame Street" which may air while dinner is being prepared.

For most children, bathtime is a relaxing and enjoyable event, and for these children an evening bath or shower is a welcome routine. However, if your child doesn't like baths, there's no reason to make him take one more often than every few days. Washing his hands and face is adequate for hygiene, and you'll avoid unnecessary hassles. All children two and over should be helped to brush their teeth in the evening.

Ideally, the bedtime routine should be quiet and low key. Children love to roughhouse and wrestle, but this kind of play may make it hard to settle down to sleep. If you want to put aside time for tumbling about, try to do it at least an hour before bedtime. One of the best routines for children is to have storytime. Children who are regularly read to by parents develop a love for reading that is the foundation for later learning. What nicer time to read than at the quiet time before sleep? Limit stories by time or by number of books, and then say goodnight. If you anticipate requests for drinks of water, blanket adjustment, or other pleas for attention, tell your child you'll come back once and that is all. If you are quietly firm, he'll learn, over time, that goodnight means goodnight.

It is also important to schedule your own bedtime. Many busy parents wait until the children are asleep to get other tasks done. It's understandable to want to have some free time in the evening, but try to set limits for yourselves. In these early months of being parents of two, it's important for your energy and moods to get enough rest. A regular bedtime is as good for you as it is for your children.

34

~~~~~~

TRAINING NUMBER ONE TO BE AN OLDER SIBLING

Once your baby is born, your first child will begin to learn—one way or another—how to be an older sibling. As a parent, you can provide her with three ways of learning:

(1) modelling the kind of behavior you want her to imitate,

(2) distracting and discouraging her from misbehavior and

(3) training her to become the kind of older sibling you would like her to be.

All three approaches are important.

Young children learn by watching their parents. Your child will notice the many ways in which you care for the baby every day. Most parents feel comfortable having the older child around while they feed or play with the baby. A few parents worry that if the older child sees them fussing over the new baby too much she will become more jealous than she might otherwise be. A mother may try to avoid giving the baby too much attention when big sister is around, or may excuse herelf every time she nurses, not out of modesty, but because she doesn't want her older child to feel left out. While understandable, this approach is not one that will help your child learn to be a caring sibling. Children are often sensitive to parents' ambivalent feelings, and your child can become confused and upset if she senses that you behave differently towards the baby whenever she is around. It's best to care for your new baby with all the love and attention you gave to your first child and to tell your older child that this is how you cared for *her* when she was a baby.

The second approach, distraction, and discouragement, will always be necessary, but misbehavior can be minimized if you plan ahead. Anticipate the older child's need for distraction by having toys or activities for him when you know the baby needs you, so that he won't annoy or misbehave out of boredom. Try to remind the older one about rules ahead of time so that you don't have to stop him after he already has broken them. Remember, most young children don't have good control over their impulses, and calm reminders can help.

The third approach, training, is not difficult, but parents should remember that training is an *ongoing* need. A parent should be like a coach who explains the rules of a game and then watches, reminds, encourages, and corrects the players during every practice. Your child needs time to learn to do everything—to be gentle, to be helpful, and to share your time and attention. He won't learn overnight.

Most young children enjoy having their parents teach them to be helpful with the new baby. Even a three-year-old can help by getting diapers, wetting a washcloth, helping to wrap the baby in a blanket, or by singing and talking to the baby. Try hard to let your child help when he wants to, but don't demand that he do so. If he resists, leave him alone. If he *always* wants to help, you might ask yourself, "Is he worried that if he *doesn't* help I will be angry or not care for him?" The average young child will have moments of misbehavior no matter how cooperative he is, so if your child is "too good" make sure that you let him know that you love him even when he's not being helpful (see Key 28).

A young child can also be taught how to stimulate a young baby to respond. Talking and singing to the baby will quiet her, and the sight of big brother's face is captivating even to a two-week-old. You can have your child sit with his face about 18 inches from the baby's at a time when she is quiet and alert. Have him slowly stick his tongue out and in, over and over. After a short while, the baby may purse her mouth and begin to stick her tongue out at him!

You can also make it your child's job to "teach the baby how to smile." Tell your child that the baby will smile when she is about a month old, and that if he talks to her and pays attention to her, he will be the first person she smiles for. If your child tries at all, he will almost certainly be there for an early smile, and you can then tell him how wonderful and important he was to help her learn to be a happy baby!

35

~~~~~~

BUILDING THE RELATIONSHIP, NOT THE RIVALRY

A ll parents want their children to be loving friends. When an older sibling begins to react negatively to the new baby, as most children do at some point, parents may be upset or angry. It may not occur to them that *their* reaction may actually promote rather than prevent sibling rivalry.

Children quite naturally have negative feelings about any big change that disrupts their lives, especially if that change includes getting less attention from parents. If your child says mean words or loses her temper with you and you tell her, "Don't talk that way," or "You mustn't feel that way," she won't stop having negative feelings. What may happen is that she will stop expressing her feelings to you because, like all young children, she fears losing your approval and love at such a critical time. Instead, she may take out her anger on the baby.

Your child needs your acceptance of her negative feelings in order for her to be able to resolve them. It's best if you can encourage her to express herself in words, even if you don't always like what she says. If she remarks, "I don't want the baby in this car," or "When is that baby going to leave?" you can respond: "It's hard to have a new baby. Sometimes we're so tired and busy we don't give you a lot of attention. We love you a lot." You don't need to apologize for having a new baby or to discount your child's reaction. You can simply accept her reaction and reassure her that you love her no matter how she feels. The more that your child feels secure with her relationship with you, the less she will need to react against the baby.

In some families, parents create negative feelings about their children's relationships by retelling what the adults think are funny stories about sibling rivalry: "Remember the time that Billy wanted to take Sarah to the recycling center?" You can create and perpetuate the idea that your children have never gotten along if you tell these stories without balancing them with stories about *nice* ways that the children have acted towards each other. Children love to hear how their little brothers followed them around like puppies, or how their big sisters used to sing to them as they fell asleep.

Be aware of the nice things your older child does for the baby, even if all you can say is, "I really like the way you were careful not to knock the baby over when you ran across the room." If your child shares a toy or simply ignores the fact that a sibling is playing with his things, tell the child how pleased you are. Show him *many times a day* what he is doing right, and he won't be devastated when you have to tell him what he is doing wrong.

Try not to compare the children. This is one of the most important rules of parenting. From the beginning, you can talk about differences and how all children are different, both inside and outside of your family. But "different" doesn't have to be "opposite." Don't label one child "active" and the other "quiet," or one "easy" and the other "difficult." If you introduce the idea that every quality in each child can be contrasted with a quality in the other sibling, you will be setting the stage for rivalry.

The "fairness" issue. One of the greatest challenges for parents of two arises when the issue of "fairness" comes up. This issue is highly charged, often because parents themselves have memories of growing up in families where they felt a parent favored one child. These parents may want to be fair with their own children in an attempt to protect them from jealous feelings. Unfortunately, it is almost impossible to be truly fair, because children don't have the same wants and needs at the same time. The pursuit of fairness can take parents down a path to a ridiculous end. One parent reported weighing out cookie dough so that none of the cookies was bigger than another. Other parents can't pick up children from school without having a negotiation about whose turn it is to sit in front.

When parents give their children the idea that adults think it is important to be fair, children will believe it too. Instead, tell your children from the beginning that you love them both, but that you aren't always going to be able to be fair. As one parent said, "Life isn't always fair, and it's not right for me to send my children out into the world thinking that it will be. In our family, when one child complains that the other has more than he does, we just say: 'You'd like it if you both could be treated exactly the same, but you are very different people. We can't always be fair, but we love you both.' "

Remember that sibling jealousy, competition, and quarreling are part of life with more than one child. Your task is not to rid your children of negative feelings, but to help them *cope* with them. Emphasize the positive aspects of your children's relationship and you will find that the rivalry is minimized.

36

~~~~~~

WHAT ABOUT MOM AND DAD?

The older child isn't the only person in your family who must adjust to the new baby. Parents, too, need to change in the way they relate to each other. In Key 31, you read how some of the changes involve getting used to the increasing complexity of communication as your family grows. There are other changes as well.

The biggest change in your relationship is easy to describe, but difficult to live with: *You and your partner will have less time to spend together.* Even if you have been careful up until now to schedule evenings out, or to arrange private time after your first child has gone to sleep, the arrival of your new baby may make it much more difficult to be alone with each other. You may find that the baby needs attention late into the evening, or that if the baby and the older child go to sleep early, one—or both—parents would rather go to sleep as well. You may find that the moments you had to catch up on each other's day no longer exist, and that you are going for days or weeks without having a real conversation. Some couples feel as though they no longer have a partner, but a coworker instead. Sometimes one or both partners can find themselves feeling angry or depressed much of the time.

It's very hard to know how to solve this kind of problem when you are in the middle of a daily struggle to get the work done, but it's important that parents find time to talk with each other. It may be helpful to think about your relationship with your partner as a kind of blueprint for your children to follow as they learn about relationships. If you were your child, watching you and your spouse, what would you be learning about parents? Would you see two people who enjoy each other's company, who are thoughtful and considerate and loving, or would you see parents who hardly talk and seem to be more concerned with housework or office work than with having fun together?

If you think your relationship as a couple could use some improvement, the first step is to take time to talk about it. If you can't leave the children or wait until they are both asleep, go on a family walk together. These walks can be a wonderful way for parents to talk. Your older child can run around and your baby will be content in a stroller or front pack. You and your partner will have some time together without the distractions of home.

Talk about your feelings, about the way life is for each of you. Try to say how you are feeling, rather than criticize your partner. It's very helpful to think, "What can each of us be doing to make our lives together more satisfying?" Is there one area that you could simplify, or one responsibility that you can set aside for now? You may think that you should still be able to stay as late at the office as you used to, or to prepare as many gourmet meals as you used to. Of course you can, but what would be the cost to your relationship?

Even if you don't come up with any permanent solutions as you talk, you will feel better for taking the time to try. If you found that the time you chose worked for you, plan another time to talk again. You could set a date and even discuss what you will talk about or what you will do. You could decide to set a goal for yourselves, such as getting a sitter for a night out or meeting for lunch. Some parents work out a weekly "date" during the day, or make family walks a regular part of the evening. Whatever you do, if it works, keep trying. If it doesn't, look for another solution, but keep working at your relationship as a couple. It is the *foundation* of your family life and the best investment you'll ever make for your children's future.

37

~~~~~~

THE BABY BECOMES A CHILD

In the first months of being the parents of two, you will probably refer to your second child as "the baby." Gradually, this little one will emerge as a full-fledged member of your family. You will see many transitions along the way and your reactions may be mixed. With your first child, you probably greeted each developmental milestone with joy, feeling pleased and proud of every new accomplishment. With your second child, particularly if you're planning to have her be your last, your joy may be tinged with sadness. Every time she grows up a little, you know that you're letting go of a moment with her that you can never recapture.

It can be tempting to try to hold back time a little with your second child. You may find yourself letting her act younger or more babyish than other children her same age. Your older sibling may be put off when you "baby" the baby, but he may also be willing for his little sister to be kept in a different category—he'll be the big kid and she can be the baby.

Of course, you may not be the sort of parent who enjoys taking care of a baby. You may be anxious right from the beginning to get through the days and nights of too many diapers and feedings, and not enough sleep. That's acceptable too, but you need to remember that babyhood is an important stage. If your older child seems more interesting and exciting, it can be tempting to spend less time talking and playing with a baby who can't do much. Try consciously to pay attention to your baby even when she's not asking for attention. Smile at her and talk to her while she's being bathed or changed, and be sure always to hold her while she's drinking her bottle, instead of propping it up. Number two will never be as wonderful as number one *unless* she keeps getting the same kind of loving attention!

No matter what you do, it won't be very long before your baby becomes a child and you will be dealing with a relationship between two children with different needs. Keys 38 through 42 will give you ideas for helping your family life run smoothly once you have two children.

38

REASONABLE EXPECTATIONS

Foremost among reasonable expectations when you are raising two children is to realize that your children will be different. This may seem obvious when you think how distinct two children's personalities can be. But your children will be dissimilar in ways you never thought about when you had only one child. For example, your new baby may nurse more often than your first, or have a less predictable mood, or be more sensitive to noise. Your children may develop at different rates, and you may worry if one child seems slower than the other. Most parents enjoy observing the differences between their children, but sometimes the characteristics of one child will worry you when you compare them to those of her sibling. You may ask for help from a pediatrician, teacher, or other parents if you find yourself worrying.

Another reasonable expectation is that you will be tired much of the time, particularly in the first few years. Part of your fatigue will result from more work and less time to sleep. Parents of two children are also less likely to take time for themselves to exercise or to eat healthy, well-balanced meals. I often suggest that a parent who is too tired to do anything else will actually feel more energetic if she takes a brisk walk every day or takes time and eats a good breakfast.

It is also reasonable to expect that your housework will increase and that you may need to make some changes in "who does what." In a great number of homes, many of the daily home-oriented tasks such as cleaning, cooking, and taking care of the children are performed primarily by the mother. If this has been the pattern in your family, and both parents feel comfortable with the arrangement, there may be no need to change. But in some families, especially when the mother is working outside the home, this division of labor becomes a problem after the birth of the second child. It can be very hard for couples to alter long-standing patterns, but it is important to discuss these issues. Women who feel overwhelmed by the demands of their families often wind up feeling depressed or resentful. Husbands are frequently very willing to make changes, if only they are asked.

Another reasonable expectation is that you and your partner will not always agree about caring for and disciplining your children. Sometimes these disagreements will be simple differences in the way you view a problem. At other times, your differences will reflect the different ways each of your parents cared for, and disciplined, you. You may also find that each of you has certain feelings about your children, perhaps because you share certain personality traits, or because your sex or order of birth is the same. When differences and disagreements occur, it is helpful to talk about them so that you can be united in your approach to the children.

It is also reasonable to expect that no matter how wonderful your children are, there will be occasions when you wish you had more time to yourself. Raising two children is hard work, and you also know that you will never get a complete vacation from the responsibility, but just some help along the way. There isn't a parent around who hasn't wondered, "Did we make a mistake?" Rest assured that you don't have to love every moment of parenting to do a good job.

One more reasonable expectation is that while your family life will be much less predictable, it will also be more exciting. In the midst of the noise—sometimes happy, sometimes quarrelsome—that is often the background music to all of your daily activity, keep in mind that what you are experiencing is a part of normal family life with two children.

39

~~~~~~

PROMOTING RESPONSIBILITY

I t is not unusual for parents—especially mothers—of two young children to feel overwhelmed by the responsibility of housework. The laundry, cooking, and general cleaning needed to maintain a semblance of order in your home requires hours of work each day. Although it may seem more efficient to wait until your children are asleep or occupied elsewhere to begin your chores, you should consider teaching your youngsters at an early age to take responsibility for helping you.

Young children are eager to imitate adults and they love to do routine, repetitive activities. Isn't that the perfect state of mind for doing housekeeping chores? Even a toddler can take the dishes out of the dishwasher for you to put away, can help pile laundry, and can even wipe up the inevitable spills. Of course, allowing and encouraging your children to help you initially will not decrease your work load—in fact, it may increase it. But if you look at the harassed parents of school-age children who are still complaining, "My kids never do anything to help," you might be motivated to get your children trained and responsible now.

Encouraging your children to take responsibility for cleaning up and doing chores begins with making them feel good about cooperating. Every time your child does a household task, be sure to *praise* him. Watch especially for the times that he helps without being asked. "Catch him being good," as the expression goes, and tell him how pleased you are.

You will need to *model* the behavior you want your children to imitate. If you want them to learn to clear the table or to pick up their clothes, you as parents need to do the same. It's particularly important for fathers to participate in household chores, especially if they have a son. If a young child sees mommy waiting on daddy, he is likely to choose to imitate daddy and expect her to wait on him, too.

In addition to modeling the behavior you want from your children, you must also *teach* it. Small children can't be expected to figure out how to do everything on their own. They need to have you show them how to hold a plate with both hands or to pour a glass of milk without spilling. As you teach them, you'll be able to see what each one is capable of doing and how much you need to modify tasks to fit the developmental abilities of each. You can then adjust your expectations accordingly. For example, the younger child can take the silverware out of the dishwasher, and the older one can sort the various pieces. The older child can help set the table, and the younger child can help clear it. Be sure to demonstrate each task as often as necessary, and don't expect perfect performances for quite a while.

After you praise, model, and teach, there's still one more important step to get your children to be responsible. Even children who like to help will only continue to do so if you are *consistent* in your expectations. You have to remind them every day to do the tasks they have learned, remembering to continue to praise and thank them for all their help.

Think of your job as being that of coach, trainer, and supervisor. Your reward, over time, will be that your two responsible children will be no more work than the single over-indulged child of some other parents. Your children's reward will come from learning about being cooperative and helpful with each other as well as with you. They will also be able to share the wonderful sibling bond of complaining about how hard their parents make them work!

40

DEALING WITH FIGHTS

From the time that your younger child becomes mobile and invades the space and possessions of your older child, the possibility of fights exists. Young children often communicate by hitting, pushing, poking, and shoving, even when they are old enough to know better.

It can be very difficult for parents to see physical fighting breaking out between children and many parents are unsure of what to do. Sometimes parents will disagree as to the best way to manage fighting. One will want to intervene to protect or punish, and the other will think it best to stay removed from the battle and let the children work it out. Your reaction to your children's fights probably will be influenced by the way you remember your own childhood and the relationships you had with your siblings and friends.

Here are some guidelines to use in deciding how to react when quarrels break out:
- Whenever possible, stay out of your children's disagreements. When you get involved, you run the risk of having your children compete for your help in becoming the "winner." Most fights are not one-sided. Sometimes the child who appears to be the "victim" has provoked the attack. Even young toddlers can learn how to get an older sibling in trouble.
- Don't let a fight continue if either child is being hit or hurt. Even if the hurt is accidental, children need to know that there are clear limits on physical interactions. You can't wait for a serious injury to occur before intervening. Ask

yourself, "Would I permit an adult to hurt my child in this way?" If the answer is no, then you shouldn't allow a child to do so either.

- If you get involved, don't try to sort out how the fight started or who is to blame. If you do, your children will get in the habit of waiting for you to come in to solve their problems instead of learning to work things out on their own.

- The best way to stop a fight and to discourage more fighting is to separate the children. You can call a five-minute time-out, and then either let them resume play together or get them involved in new activities. If the children are fighting over a toy, you can remove the toy for the day, or ask them to figure out a fair way to share.

- If you find you cannot keep your children from roughhousing, help them to learn how to play rough and tumble in a fair way. Some children are more physical than others. Little boys, especially, can enjoy playing like puppies, even if one is bigger than the other. Of course, if children are wrestling, even in fun, one of them may still get hurt. You will have to balance this risk with the difficulty of keeping them from wrestling at all.

- Be clear about your own standards for arguments. If you do not allow any expression of aggression, you may be setting yourself up for problems. You can establish limits about the type of words that you permit children to use and the type of physical contact that is allowed, but you can't reasonably expect your children to be nice all of the time. Try using the communication skills described in Key 42 to help your children work through conflict and express anger without having to hurt someone else.

- Help your children to "blow off steam" on their own. Sometimes children fight because they want to feel powerful and have no other way to express themselves. You can help to prevent confrontation by giving your children opportunities to run and climb and play outdoors every day. Children can play with squirt guns or spray bottles to have safe "battles." If you have to stay indoors, find ways to allow your children to be active. Let them jump, or hit pillows, or knock down blocks. Some families even buy a punching bag to attack, and then discover that the adults enjoy using it too!

- If you find that your children are fighting physically almost every day, step back and look at their overall pattern of interaction. You may discover that, despite the fighting, your children get along pretty well most of the time. If that is the case, look at the times when they aren't fighting, and try to figure out why they are playing together so well. There may be only certain situations or circumstances that provoke fights, and you can work to change these. Look carefully at the amount of time you are spending with your children, together and separately. Sometimes children's fights are a plea for more attention from parents.

- If your children seem to be fighting and quarreling almost all of the time, it's a good idea to do some extra reading and perhaps talk to someone outside of your family for assistance. You may also want to look at your own style of dealing with stress and anger. Do your children see you come home angry from your own day, complaining or shouting at your partner or at them? Sometimes children's behavior is an imitation of what they see in their parents. If you or your children are getting "stuck" in a pattern that makes you concerned or unhappy, try to change that pattern for their sakes as well as your own.

41

UNDERSTANDING
STAGES OF
DEVELOPMENT

When you were planning your family, you probably hoped that your children would be great playmates and, someday, close friends. Unfortunately, even if your children, as a rule, play well together, it is likely that there will be times when they seem unable to get along at all—with each other or even with you. You may worry, "If they can't be in the same room together without fighting, how will they ever be friends later?" It can be helpful to look at your children's behavior in the context of their current ages and stages of development. In this Key you will find some guidelines to typical behavior seen at various ages of young children. Remember that children develop at different rates, so that the behavior described for each age group may not match what you see in your own child.

In any family, all siblings, unless they are twins, are always at different stages of development. It may help you to take some of their conflicts and misbehavior in stride if you remind yourself of what you can reasonably expect from each child at any time.

Infants

During his first six months or life, your baby will need to follow his own schedule, and the household will have to adapt to his needs. An older child who has needs of his own will often feel that it isn't fair that he must wait when the baby doesn't, or that the family must accommodate the baby's naps and meals.

As the baby gets older, he will be awake more and more. Although he may be more fun for the older child, who will certainly enjoy interacting with him, the infant will also start to demand more attention from the entire family. If your baby is cute and sociable, he may get lots of comments and friendly looks from others. Your older child may then feel as though his own arena is being intruded upon.

As the baby becomes mobile, you will have to childproof your living areas. Your older child may feel proud and grown-up about having different safety rules from the baby, but he may also feel resentful if he is not allowed to be as messy with his toys as before.

The worst times come when the baby is active enough to crawl or pull himself up to the places where your older one has left his carefully arranged toys. As block towers tumble, so may your visions of children playing together in harmony. However, this stage is only temporary.

Toddlers

Toddlers are one- to two-year-olds who are fully mobile but still can't talk very well. They often feel frustrated at not being able to express themselves, and this frustration can erupt in tantrums. Older children can be upset by tantrums, probably because they have strong feelings of their own that they are trying to keep contained.

Toddlers are also at an age when they want to learn about the world. They learn best by exploring, touching, tasting, and looking. They learn only a little by listening to a parent or sibling. They are eager to do things by themselves, but since they aren't very skilled, they continually make messes and mistakes. Parents and siblings alike can become upset when they are victims of a toddler's innocent destructiveness. One- and two-year-olds don't understand the reasons for rules, although they *can* follow the rules if they are consistently applied over and over again.

Last, but perhaps most challenging of all, toddlers are trying very hard to assert their independence from their parents. They will pull away and be oppositional—until they scare themselves by their own desire to be independent and collapse into clinginess and whining.

With this description, you can see that if either of your children is in this stage of development, you will have your hands full. If you can view it as typical toddler behavior rather than misbehavior between siblings or a reaction to the new baby, you will be able to get through this stage much more easily.

Threes

Three-year-olds generally are pretty delightful and easygoing compared to two-year-olds. They have much better verbal skills and can listen to and follow directions fairly well. They enjoy being coooperative and like to please. They can play well for at least a half hour on their own, staying busy with toys and imaginary games.

However, they are also self-centered and can't see the world from any point of view but their own. They are busy with their own activities and don't like to be interrupted, although they see no reason not to interrupt anyone else. They can be especially reluctant to end one activity and begin another, so transition times can be troublesome. It's quite common for three-year-olds to be difficult when it is time to get dressed, leave the house, or go anywhere, including to bed at night.

A child at this stage can be very compatible with a baby, because she may really enjoy being a "big girl" (mother) playing with her (own) little baby. However, parents may find that the constant demands of an infant make them want to expect more grown-up and better behavior from the three-year-old.

If rules are carefully made and followed, most three-year-olds will be fairly dependable and cooperative. However, you can't expect them to figure out how you want them to behave unless you offer clear and consistent guidance.

Fours

The typical four-year-old can be a real challenge to parents. Although four-year-olds are better able to express themselves and are more socially skilled than younger children, it can often seem as though their overall behavior is worse. Four-year-olds often are stubborn and rebellious. A parent may wonder, "What have I done wrong?" especially when this behavior starts right about the time a new baby is born. If you talk to other parents—with or without second children—you'll probably find that your child is acting just like theirs.

Four-year-olds seem to have a need to assert themselves, perhaps because they are balanced between the little babies and toddlers who can't do very much and the stronger, self-confident older children that they admire and envy. Fours act up because they feel so small. They play superheroes, have elaborate games, and run imaginary households where they can feel powerful. As the parent of a four-year-old, you will have to set firm limits, at the same time remembering that he is acting tough because deep down he feels helpless. Fortunately, with a baby in the house, he knows that he is no longer the smallest person at home.

42

COMMUNICATION SKILLS

PeOple communicate in many ways. Most of the time we are communicating information. We tell others what we did that day, or what we're having for dinner, or how to complete a task. Most of us do a pretty good job of exchanging the information we need to go about our daily lives.

Exchanging information is one kind of communication. Another kind of communication occurs when we talk about our feelings. You may have had the experience of telling someone about how you felt and having them listen to you in a way that made you feel that they understood and accepted what you said. If so, you know how good it can feel to communicate in that way. Similarly, you can learn to listen to your children in a way that makes them want to talk to you and helps them to feel that you understand. In this Key you will find suggestions for building communication skills with your children.

If you want to have good communication with your children, you have to take time to be with them. As you may have noticed, children won't talk on schedule. They don't volunteer much when you ask them direct questions, even when the question is, What did you do today? There are certain times when a child is more likely to open up. If you can create times when you are together and there are moments of silence, he will often begin to share his thoughts with you. Some good opportunities are:

- in the evening at bedtime
- when you are driving in the car, especially with the radio off
- when you are sitting and waiting in a restaurant or the doctor's office
- when you go for a walk together.

Look at your daily life and see where some quiet moments can be worked in to give your child a chance to talk.

When your child does talk, focus on *listening*. Don't think about what you are going to say and don't worry about making it a two-way conversation. Many times your child will be satisfied just knowing that you listened. As you listen, pay attention to his words, his facial expression, and the tone of his voice.

As your child talks, you can keep the conversation going by echoing and repeating what he says. It may feel artificial at first, but after you see how effective this response can be, you will find it easier to use. Let's look at an example. If your child comes home from school and you ask, "What did you do this morning?" he may say, "We played in the yard." If you then say, "Did you have fun?" he is likely to reply, "Yes." At that point you probably will find yourself saying, "What else did you do?" and he will either answer, "Nothing," or name another activity. After a few more questions you will probably both stop talking. Another approach would be the following:

Child: "We played in the yard today."
Parent: "Oh, you played in the yard?"
Child: "Yes, we played on the climbing structure."
Parent: "You played on the climbing structure?"
Child: "Yes, me and Matt."
Parent: "You and Matt played together on the climbing structure."

117

Child: "Yes, except Matt didn't want to play what I wanted
    to play."
Parent: "He didn't?"
Child: "No, he wanted to play with David."

You can see that even though the parent's responses are very restrained, they can cue a child to keep going.

As you listen to your child, pay attention to what might be going on for him emotionally as he talks. At an appropriate time you can respond to what you think he might be feeling as well as to the words he uses. To continue the above conversation:

Parent: "It sounds as if you didn't like it that Matt wanted to
    play with David."
Child: "He wanted to play with David and we weren't done
    with our game."
Parent: "It made you sad that he didn't want to finish your
    game."
Child: "Yeah."

This could be the end of the conversation, but your child would probably feel that you had listened well and that you understood what he was thinking and feeling. Most conversations with children last only a few minutes, but a lot can happen in that time to increase the bond of communication between you.

If your child wanted to continue to talk you could keep listening and echoing his words and feelings. You could also try to rephrase one of his remarks.

Child: "That David is really a dummy."

At this point you might be tempted to say, "Don't call David a dummy. That's not a nice thing to say." Instead, try:

Parent: "David didn't want to play the game that you wanted to play."

Child: "He's really stupid."

Parent: "You really get angry when you think about David."

Child: "Yes, I wish he'd just go away."

Parent: "If he went away you could play with Matt all by yourself."

Child: "Yes. I really wish he'd leave us alone."

The conversation may end here, but if your child still seems interested in talking, you can help him think about the problem that is bothering him. Most children don't like to be given advice or instructions about how they should feel, but perhaps they can accept your ideas if you begin with the phrase, "Some kids . . ."

Parent: "Some kids get sad and angry when other kids don't want to play with them."

Child: "Yes. Benji was really angry at Alex today."

Parent: [Echoing again] "Benji was angry at Alex?"

Child: "Yes, Alex wanted to play with trucks and Benji wanted him to play with Legos."

Parent: "Sometimes kids have to find someone else to play with."

Child: "Yes, Alex came outside to play with us."

By talking about "other kids" you can often give your child some ideas about managing a situation without directly giving him advice. Telling stories or reading books about children or animals that have to solve problems is also an effective way of offering your child indirect assistance.

As you talk to your child, let him know that you understand how he feels.

Parent: "It sounds as if you had a hard time today. It must
      have been rough."
Child: "No, it was O.K."

If you acknowledge your child's feelings, he may be able to
accept them and move on quickly, knowing that the parents
he loves and respects understand him.

Communication skills—like all skills—have to be
learned. If you remember feeling that your parents really
understood you, then they probably had good communication
skills themselves. If you don't feel that way, you may want
to increase your own skills so that your children will be able
to express themselves better to you and to each other. Many
communities offer classes such as Parent Effectiveness Training that can help you gain the ability to "talk so kids will
listen, and listen so kids will talk." See the suggested reading
list on page 146 for books on building communication skills
on your own.

43

RETURNING TO WORK

M ore than half the women in the United States with children under one year of age in the 1990s will be employed outside of the home. If you are planning to be a family of working parents with two children, you won't be alone. In fact, you'll be part of the majority.

Despite the statistics, our society does not offer a great deal of support for working parents. The United States, unlike most other Western democratic nations, does not guarantee a woman maternity leave. For many women, time off with a new baby is limited to accumulated vacation and sick time. Most working women are back on the job by the time their newborns are three months old.

If you plan to return to work during your second baby's first year, you will have two challenges. First, you will have to find child care that works well for two children of different ages. Second, you will have to find ways to organize your time at the beginning and end of each day and on your days off to get the most out of the moments with your children.

Many working parents find that they can successfully manage the demands of careers and families. Their success comes from arranging their priorities to make time for the things they care about most. Time and energy go to the areas of highest value. If that means letting go of chores, activities, or interests that used to be important, they make that decision. Even though the parents' time with their children may be limited, the children feel comfortable knowing that there will always be times when they can count on their parents' full attention.

In Keys 44 and 45 you will find guidelines for choosing child care and for managing your time with your family once you return to work.

44

CHILD CARE CHOICES

Once you have decided to return to work, you'll have to make arrangements for child care. You've already been through the process once, but that doesn't mean it is easier the second time around. Choosing child care that works for you means, first, taking time to decide what kind of child care situation is most practical for your needs and for your children's ages. Second, you will need to evaluate the quality of care before and after your children begin the new situation.

The first decision you will have to make is, What kind of care is most suitable for our family? Your choices may include having a sitter at your home, a convenient but often expensive alternative; small-family day care, where both of your children can go to the same homelike setting; or a day care center, which is larger, but has the advantage of having professionally trained and supervised staff and sometimes a more stimulating environment for the older preschooler. In choosing the setting that works best for you, you should consider the needs of your children in terms of their ages and stages of development.

The most important need that a baby has is for constant and consistent care. Babies need a routine that is flexible and adaptable to their own individual needs for sleep, feeding, and play. A low caregiver-to-infant ratio is essential—no more than three children under two years of age should be cared for by one individual. Consider that a home-based setting, either yours or the sitter's, has the advantage in that the sitter is better able to care for your baby when the infant is sick.

It is, unfortunately, inevitable that a baby with an older sibling will have several colds or other illnesses during the first year of life, and you will either need to take off from work or have a sitter or substitute available to take care of the sick child.

Toddlers need the same kind of consistent and attentive care that babies do, but they also need a caregiver who understands their need to explore and carry out their own ideas and interests. They need someone who can help them understand about limits as they learn to assert themselves as individuals. A sitter who is wonderful with a baby may not have the skills to entertain and discipline an active and inquisitive toddler, so it is important to ask ahead of time whether she has had experience with both age groups.

Children who are three years of age and older benefit from being with other children their own age. They are ready for activities such as art projects, music, cooking, and dramatic as well as imaginary play. They also need space to run and climb. A preschool-age child who is in a setting that is too confining or boring will often misbehave as a way of keeping life interesting. If he always has to pace his energy to the schedule of a baby, you may find that he is acting aggressively and is angry much of the time.

In the beginning, you may find a setting that can provide care for both of your children. If so, you will have two advantages: convenience for yourselves as parents, plus an opportunity for your children to play together and get to know one another without having to compete for your attention. Sometimes siblings can form an especially close relationship with one another as their bond grows stronger in their parents' absence. However, if your children are in care together and you find that one child seems to be forming a closer relationship with the provider than the other, you need to reevaluate your choice of child care. It may be that the sitter prefers one child and is not paying enough attention to the other. This kind of long-term discrimination can be very damaging to the child who is left out, and the sibling relationship will suffer as each child begins to feel angry or guilty about the imbalanced situation.

If you decide to take your children to different places for care, you will be able to match the needs of each child with what that setting has to offer. However, you'll also need to provide time for your children to develop their own relationship since they won't be together most of the time. See Key 45 for suggestions for managing time as a working family.

As you analyze your child care choices, it is important to look at safety, supervision, organization, equipment, and the background of the provider. Always ask for references and check them. Ask your pediatrician for guidelines or read some books or pamphlets about evaluating child care. It isn't enough to trust that the provider "must know what she's doing." Providing quality child care demands skill and intelligence, no matter what the formal training of the caregiver may be. Now that you have two children, the demands on your time and energy will make it even harder to do the research and evaluation necessary to find good care, but there's no way to avoid it if you want your children to have the best.

45

~~~~~~

MAKING TIME
FOR TWO

Time. There never seems to be enough of it. Ask working parents with two children what they need most and at least one of them will say, "Two more hours in every day." Like many parents, you will have bills to pay, and work that may not allow you the luxury of staying home part or full time, even if you wanted to. Your busy schedules may make you feel as though you are racing through your days without taking time to enjoy yourselves or your children.

If you are feeling this frustration, your children may be feeling the same way. Young children would rather be with their parents than with anyone else, no matter how much they love the people who care for them while you are away. With two children needing your time and attention, you have even greater demands to meet. Fortunately, young children are fairly resilient, and they will adjust to your absence and in most cases cope well with the amount of time you have available for them. But if your time is limited, make sure that it is well spent.

The beginning and end of each workday is often stressful, as you ready your children in the morning and reconnect with them in the evening. You have places to get to, but your children are reluctant to "switch gears" just because the clock tells you they have to. Often parents find themselves engaged in struggles, with quarrels and tears on all sides. You can ease these times a bit by planning ahead. Try to streamline the morning routine and allow yourselves time to say goodbye gradually. Many children will skim through breakfast and getting dressed if they know that Mom or Dad is going to tell them a story in the car or help them get settled with a project at the child care center.

The time when you pick up your children is equally important. Take a moment to chat with your caregiver about how the day went. A caregiver who feels that you value her relationship with your children will be better able to help, especially if problems arise. Many children are helped through the transition to home by having a small snack on the walk or ride home. Once home, try to hold off on your desire to read the mail, start dinner, and unwind from the day. Instead, take fifteen minutes to settle in, giving your children all of your attention, with a story or a short cuddle. You may not feel you can make time for this, but parents who try this technique often discover that, after giving this initial attention to their children, the rest of the evening goes more smoothly.

Many working parents find that the evening hours can be a hectic blur as they get through the chores they need to finish before the next day begins. Sometimes a parent will feel pressure because of an idealized image of what "Supermoms" and "Superdads" supposedly accomplish—cooking gourmet meals while Vivaldi plays on the stereo and the three-year-old practices reading French flashcards! Of course, these are just fantasies, but if you're eating frozen pizza in a cluttered kitchen while the children throw food on the floor, it can be hard to imagine a middle ground. If possible, streamline and simplify mealtime, using prepared foods (by you or someone else) and sticking to the foods your children like to eat. Save special dishes for the weekend or lunches out.

Whatever your children's bedtime, it's important to have a routine for each child. Bedtime is the time when children most need the comfort and security of familiar faces and patterns. A bath, story, cuddle, and quiet talk can be accomplished in a half hour. It's much better to have a short routine that you repeat every night than a more elaborate series of activities that can take place only when you aren't too tired or busy. If you have to be out in the evening, it is then easier for a sitter to follow a short routine and substitute for you.

Try to cut back on social obligations so that you have time with your family on weekends. It may be hard for parents to engage in "kid stuff" with their children during their spare days off, but that's what the youngsters really enjoy. Even if you don't relish the thought of a Saturday at Totland, the time you spend relaxing with your children while they are young is money in the bank for your future relationship together. Older children and teens are drawn to spending time with their friends, not their parents. If your children don't have many years of happy memories of family time to compete with the attractions of their peers, you may see very little of them as they grow up.

Working parents are sometimes told that "quality time" is more important than "quantity time"—the amount of time actually spent with children. Sometimes the expression quality time is interpreted to mean that if parents spend limited moments with their children engaged in stimulating, entertaining, or educational activities, the children will be fine. Not so. Special activities are fun, but they are extras. Children need quantity time too—every day—from the people they love most. By being available to your children for as many of their small moments as you can, you provide them with the security that all children deserve, whether you work at home or outside the home.

46

ADOPTING A
SECOND CHILD

amilies are different in many ways. If one or both of
your children came to you by adoption, you will find
that you have to pay special attention to some issues in
your family that are different from the issues in other families.
In any family, the arrival of a new baby causes the older child
to wonder about many things, such as, "Where do babies come
from?" and "Is the new baby going to take my parents' love
and attention away from me?" As an adoptive family, your
ways of dealing with your child's questions and concerns will
be somewhat different from those of other families.

If your first child is also adopted, you probably have
already told him so. If not, it is important that you do so as
soon as possible. However, even if you have talked about
being adopted, he may not really understand what that means.
Since young children have a limited understanding of reproduction, the difference between the mother who gave birth
and the mother who is raising him may be confusing.

At some point, you should tell your child that all babies
grow inside a mother, and that he and the new baby grew
inside a mother just like every other child. You can tell him
that his birth mother and the new baby's birth mother were
not able to take care of a baby, and so they found your family
to take care of the babies and keep them for their own. The
important concepts for your child to undertand are that he
was a baby just like every other baby and that there was

nothing different about him. He also needs to hear that his birth mother was someone who could not take care of a baby—*any* baby, not just him—and so she made sure that he would be cared for. You need to make it very clear to your child that when you adopted him, you adopted him forever and that he will always be your child. Otherwise, he may think that if one mother could give him up, another one might, too.

If your first child is not adopted, he will still need explanations about the different ways that babies become part of a family and about the way that the new baby came to you. It is particularly important for him to know that the new baby is going to stay with your forever. It is common for older children to want to return their biological siblings to wherever they came from, so you should anticipate that you will get the same suggestion about your adopted baby.

All children need to feel secure in their parents' love. Most older children go through periods of insecurity when a new baby comes into the family. As adoptive parents, you need to pay special attention to the ways in which your child expresses worries or anxieties. Children who are adopted may start thinking about what you have told them about their birth and may ask new questions or repeat questions they asked in the past.

Make use of their renewed interest by telling them again the story of their birth and arrival in your family. Most children like to hear stories about themselves over and over again, and each time you tell him the story, you reach your child at new levels, as he understands more each time. The explanations you give when he is three can be adjusted as he grows older. Just as it is important to explain reproduction many times as a child grows up, it is important to explain and reexplain adoption.

As parents, you will deal with some issues with your adopted child or children that may come as a surprise to you. In every family, parents will at times feel differently towards their children. This is especially true if one child is easier to care for than another, or has traits that a parent finds more attractive. Most parents feel worried or guilty about sometimes preferring one child over another, not realizing that these feelings are normal. In an adoptive family, you may find that these feelings worry you even more. Discussing your feelings with your partner or someone outside your family can be helpful.

Adoptive families will find that there are many community resources that can assist them in meeting the special needs of their children. See the suggested reading list at the back of this book for further references.

47

IF THE NEW BABY IS PREMATURE OR SICK

I f your new baby is born too early or has a problem at birth, your family life will be disrupted in many ways. All of the planned changes in your lives will be put on hold while your baby's well-being is uncertain.

It is normal for you to want to direct all your attention and concern towards the child who is sick. You may want to spend most of your time at the hospital, either staying with the baby, meeting with doctors and nurses, or just waiting. If the baby is taken to a regional medical center some distance from your home, you will spend much time in travel and may even need to spend the night away from home.

If you are faced with this situation, it will be hard for you to pay a lot of attention to your older child. While you are home, you may feel distracted and worried much of the time. Many of the suggestions in the earlier Keys for easing sibling adjustment will be difficult or impossible for you to follow. There is no way that you can take care of everyone's emotional needs during a time of stress such as this, but you can learn to cope. In this Key you will find guidelines for coping with the stress of having both a premature or sick baby and an older child who needs you.

• Ask friends and family for help. It's important to have people you trust who can be supportive and help out with your home life. Friends and neighbors are usually willing to help with meals and errands, but you may have to ask.

- Request a friend or family member to pay special attention to your older child and to spend time with him as often as possible. If you are unavailable at times, that person can be the steady source of security your child will need if he is feeling lonely.

- Explain to your child what is wrong with the new baby, even if someone else has told him first. Be as truthful as you can, but if he asks questions you can't answer, it's all right to say, "I don't know." Ask your child if he knows why the baby has a problem. He may be feeling, as many children do, that something he said or did caused the baby to be early or sick. It's important to reassure him that the baby's difficulties are not his fault. Don't be surprised, however, if your child doesn't act concerned about the baby's problems. Young children are self-centered by nature, and your child's major worry may be how the new baby's condition affects *him.*

- If your child asks whether the baby is going to die, tell him that the doctors and nurses at the hospital are doing everything they can to make the baby well. Try not to promise that the baby will be healthy soon. From a child's point of view, even a few weeks is a long time.

- Take a picture of the new baby to show to your child, and be ready to explain why the baby looks small or sick. Tell him about the tubes and machines and the special crib the baby is in. Take a picture of your child and tape it to the baby's crib with the words: "I'm Billy's baby sister."

- If the baby is in stable condition and the hospital will permit it, consider taking your older child to visit the new baby. Although the intensive care nursery can be a frightening place to children (and adults!), it may be less scary than what he is imagining. The nurses may be able to help your child understand what is happening to his baby sister and he may be able to touch or hold his new sibling. This experience can be the beginning of a caring, loving attachment between your children.

- Try to keep your older child's life as stable and routine as possible. Even if you spend much of your time at the hospital, try to have one parent at home for your child's bedtime and for when he wakes up in the morning. Don't plan a lot of "special" activities to make up for your absence. Your child will be better off if he can feel that some of his life is going on just as usual even if other parts are not.

When the baby is ready to leave the hospital, review the earlier Keys and start off as if you have just come home with a brand-new infant. You probably will find that your older child quickly forgets that he's been longing for his sister to come home, as he starts acting and reacting like any older sibling who has to cope with a new arrival. You'll need to prepare him for the baby's special needs, which may include more frequent feeding, carrying, and comforting than the average newborn requires. Your time will be filled, but don't forget to ease your older child into his new role as you adjust to yours.

48

~~~~~~

WHEN THE NEW BABY IS A HALF-SIBLING

Families are changing, and more and more children in this country are experiencing divorce and remarriage by one or both of their parents. In many of these remarriages, parents will decide to have more children. The term "blended family" has been coined to describe the many different configurations that result from remarriage, especially when both adults have children from previous relationships. In this Key, you will find guidelines for managing the difficult challenge of becoming a family of "yours, mine, and ours."

The older child in a *blended family* can experience the same feelings of loss and displacement of her parents' attention that any child does when a new baby is born. However, she may also feel that the new arrival puts an end to her secret wish that her biological parents will one day remarry. This wish is very common in young children, though it is often not spoken. For this reason, parents of half-siblings must be especially watchful for signs of anger or sadness in an older child, either during the mother's pregnancy or after the birth. By using the communication skills described in Key 42, you can help your child express her feelings. Although you won't be able to "fix" the situation in the way your child might wish, she will feel much better if she knows that you can accept and understand her feelings.

Parents may also face some unexpected problems in their own relationship with the birth of "ours." The stepparent often takes a secondary role to the biological parent in child-rearing responsibility. With the birth of a new baby who "belongs" to both, parents may have to shift the balance of care and decision making. A parent who has held back on involvement may suddenly want to be more involved. The other parent may feel as though his or her role is being undermined. The older child may feel as though her stepparent loves the new baby more because of this increased involvement.

The shift of care and responsibility can be subtle and yet complex. There is no easy way to predict your feelings or reactions. However, it is possible to anticipate that these shifts may occur. Parents can talk about how they see their roles during pregnancy and then again after the baby arrives. When parents talk openly, the stress of the changing balance of care is minimized.

If your older child is in a shared custody situation, you have probably gotten used to helping her make the transitions between households. Once the new baby arrives, you may find that the transition times become more difficult for all of you. Your child will have to adjust to a change in the way the household functions in response to the baby. You will have to shift your attention from the ongoing needs of the baby to the needs of your other child. You may feel torn between your desire to care for one instead of the other. Mothers, especially, often report feeling guilty and unable to satisfy anyone's needs.

All the suggestions in the Keys for managing sibling reactions will be helpful to parents of half-siblings as well. However, because the blending of families can be complicated, it is often important to obtain guidance during this time of transition. Many families say that talking with other families, informally or in parent support groups, or meeting with a counselor experienced in these issues can improve family communication and prevent problems from becoming unmanageable.

QUESTIONS AND ANSWERS

Our three-year-old has started to carry her baby blanket around with her much of the time. She's been doing this ever since our baby was born two months ago. Should we make her stop?

Your child is behaving very appropriately for a new big sister. Many children react to the birth of a new baby by acting babyish or younger than they really are. If you accept her behavior, over time she will need her comfort item less.

We'll be having our baby in a local hospital that allows children to visit. Is it a good idea to bring a rambunctious two-year-old to the hospital even if it is permitted?

It's a very good idea to bring your child to see his mom as soon as he can. He needs to see that she is OK and hasn't abandoned him for the new baby. If the hospital allows children to visit, you can be sure that they are used to rambunctious two-year-olds!

In my first pregnancy, I had a lot of morning sickness that lasted all day. What should I tell my older child if I'm sick during this pregnancy?

If you aren't feeling well, let your child know that you need time to rest. You can tell her that you will be better soon, and that if you can't take care of her someone else will.

If you are too tired or sick to supervise your child, be sure to get someone else to watch her.

My children have their own rooms but the three-year-old wants the baby to sleep with him. What should we tell him?

Many children like to share a room with a sibling. The only disadvantage to sharing a room is that one child may wake the other from naps or during the night. You can try the arrangement out and see if it works for you.

My two-year-old nursed until he was eighteen months old. Will he be jealous when he sees the new baby nursing?

Your two-year-old probably will be very curious about nursing, but he is more likely to be jealous of the time and attention the baby gets from you during feeding time than the nursing itself. Be sure to have toys or books on hand to entertain him every time you need to nurse.

My two little boys always are competing to be first. Is that because they are both boys?

Your children are behaving like normal siblings. Most brothers and sisters compete for being first or best. You can't stop the competition, but you don't have to get involved in it either. Try not to get hooked into any disagreements and let them work things out on their own.

How can I protect the new baby from our older child's germs? I'm worried that we'll have two sick kids all winter.

Second children are more likely to get sick at a younger age than first children do. The good news is that they build up their immune systems earlier and you will be dealing with less illness after a few years. You can protect the baby by having everyone in the household wash hands before touching her, and by keeping your older child away if he is actively coughing and sneezing.

My wife and I disagree about some of the rules for our children. How important is it that we be consistent?

Most parents have different approaches to child rearing, and children can benefit from seeing that there is more than one way to handle a problem. Parents should decide which rules are important to enforce consistently—safety rules, for example—and which ones can be left up to the parent in charge. For times when you are together, you must work out a solution that sets a good example for your children about compromising.

How can I get both my children to nap at the same time? One is three months old and the other is two years old.

Although you can structure a two-year-old's nap schedule by being consistent in your routines, you can't expect a three-month-old to nap when you want her to. Some infants are more predictable than others, but a young baby's sleep needs generally are variable and nap time may shift slightly from day to day. As the baby gets closer to six months old you can begin to plan for a morning and afternoon nap and you may be able to coordinate the time with your older child's schedule.

Ever since our second baby was born my wife and I have been unable to get away from the children to have time for ourselves. My wife says that it is too hard to get a sitter, but it's also very hard on us. Is this what life is like with two children?

Many couples with two young children get in the habit of not making time for themselves. Unfortunately, not spending time as a couple can lead to problems in your relationship. In the long run, it's better for your children to have parents with a healthy marriage. If you want to have time away from your children, don't ask your wife to make the arrangements. Find a reliable sitter, friend, or family member who can care for the children while the two of you go off alone.

We're hoping to adopt a second child, but we don't know when. Should we be talking to our three-year-old about our plans?

Your three-year-old does not have the ability to understand why you would have to wait to adopt a baby, and his concept of time is very limited. It would be better to wait until the baby arrives to explain how he or she joined your family. However, this is a good time to begin talking about adoption in general. If your first child is adopted as well, he is ready to hear about how he joined your family.

Our second child was premature and very sick. She is home with us now but requires much more care than the average baby. How can we help our older child cope?

An older child with a new sibling needs extra time and attention under any circumstances. In your situation, your new baby is demanding so much that you can't expect to have a lot of energy for your first child as well. Try to find a family member or friend who can provide your child with some regular nurturing even when you are overwhelmed with the baby's needs. See if you can make time every day to cuddle and play with your child, even if it's just for a few minutes. Let him know that this is a hard time for all of you, and that you miss being able to be with him as much as before.

I feel very guilty about this, but I'm enjoying my new baby a lot more than I do my two-year-old. My older child is so demanding now and the baby seems easy by comparison.

A two-year-old is demanding under any circumstances, and your child may be feeling upset by the baby's arrival and consequently demanding even more from you. As hard as it may be, take some time away from the new baby to spend alone with your older child. Don't be too hard on yourself for enjoying the baby more, but don't forget that he will be a demanding two-year-old someday as well.

Our first child had colic and we had three months of misery. We're expecting a second baby now, and friends tell us not to worry because second children are easier. Is this true?

Second children are not necessarily easier but many mothers and fathers find that it is easier to take care of a second child because the parents are more experienced. Your second baby may have colic as well, but this time you will know that both you and the baby will survive. You're less likely to blame yourselves or to feel guilty. Your work may seem easier, even though the tasks haven't changed.

Ever since our baby was born, our son has been carrying around a baby doll and spending a lot of time feeding, dressing, and playing with it. Is this normal for a boy?

It's very normal for any child to reenact through play what he observes going on in real life. If your son is watching his mother and father care for a baby, he quite naturally will

142

want to play with a baby doll himself. Some boys aren't given a chance to play with dolls, because parents think that dolls are not masculine toys. As more and more dads are now involved in caring for babies, it should become more acceptable for little boys to play Daddy by taking care of a baby doll.

GLOSSARY

After pains a cramping sensation in the uterus felt by women following the birth of a second baby. The pains are caused by the contractions of the myeoepithelial cells in the uterine wall that respond to the release of the hormone oxytocin. Because oxytocin is released during breast-feeding, after pains often are felt while a woman is nursing.

Caesarean birth (sometimes called "Caesarean section" or "C-section). The delivery of a baby through an incision in the mother's uterus, through the abdominal wall. Caesarean operations are performed when medical personnel believe that a vaginal birth will put the infant or mother at risk. The term is derived from the belief, probably inaccurate, that Julius Caesar was born in this way.

Cognitive the mental process of learning and understanding.

Depression feelings of sadness, emptiness, and lack of interest in activities that previously were engaging. Prolonged depression, especially if it appears to be an excessive response to an external event, should be evaluated by a mental health professional.

Development the act of growing or expanding. In children, development occurs both gradually and in spurts. Development can be physical, cognitive, or emotional.

Miscarriage the death of a fetus (immature baby) occuring before the baby is old enough to survive outside the mother's uterus.

Oppositional behavior combative or contrary responses to parents from children. The behavior typically is seen in children who are learning to be independent.

Postpartum the recovery period following childbirth, usually defined as three months after the date of birth.

Premature an infant born earlier than 36 weeks of pregnancy, often needing special medical care because of its size or immaturity.

Regression the normal "going backwards" movement of a young child's development, usually seen following the birth of a sibling.

Sibling a brother or sister.

VBAC—Vaginal Birth After Caesarean the practice of allowing a woman to attempt a vaginal birth, under close medical supervision, after a previous Caesarean birth.

SUGGESTED READING
FOR PARENTS

Bernstein, Anne C. *Yours, Mine, and Ours: How Families Change When Remarried Parents Have a Child Together.* New York: W. W. Norton, 1989.

Brazelton, T. Berry. *Working and Caring.* Reading, Massachusetts: Addison Wesley, 1985.

Faber, Adele, and Mazlish, Elaine. *How to Talk So Kids Will Listen & Listen So Kids Will Talk.* New York: Avon Books, 1982.

————. *Siblings Without Rivalry.* New York: Avon, 1988.

Melina, Lois Ruskai. *Making Sense of Adoption.* New York: Harper and Row, 1989.

INDEX

147

DR. BALTER'S STEPPING STONE STORIES

Dr. Lawrence Balter,
Illustrations by Roz Schanzer

Each of the storybooks in this series deals with a particular concern a young child might have about growing up. Each book features the same cast of characters—the kids who live in the fictional town of Crescent Canyon, a group to whom any youngster can relate. The stories are thoroughly entertaining while they help kids to understand their own feelings and the feelings of others. Engaging full-color illustrations fill every page! (Ages 3–7) Each book: Hardcover, $5.95, 40 pp., 8" x 8"

A Funeral for Whiskers:
Understanding Death ISBN: 6153-5

A.J.'s Mom Gets a New Job:
Adjusting to a Separation ISBN: 6151-9

Alfred Goes to the Hospital: Understanding
a Medical Emergency ISBN: 6150-0

Linda Saves the Day:
Understanding Fear ISBN: 6117-9

Sue Lee's New Neighborhood:
Adjusting to a New Home ISBN: 6116-0

Sue Lee Starts School:
Adjusting to School ISBN: 6152-7

The Wedding: Adjusting to a
Parent's Remarriage ISBN: 6118-7

What's the Matter With A.J.?:
Understanding Jealousy ISBN: 6119-5

ISBN PREFIX: 0-8120

Books may be purchased at your bookstore, or by mail from Barron's. Enclose check or money order for total amount plus sales tax where applicable and 10% for postage and handling (minimum charge $1.75, Canada $2.00). Prices are subject to change without notice.

Barron's Educational Series, Inc.
250 Wireless Boulevard
Hauppauge, NY 11788
Call toll-free: 1-800-645-3476
In NY: 1-800-257-5729

IN CANADA:
Georgetown Book Warehouse
34 Armstrong Avenue
Georgetown, Ontario L7G 4R9
Call toll-free: 1-800-247-7160

BARRON'S

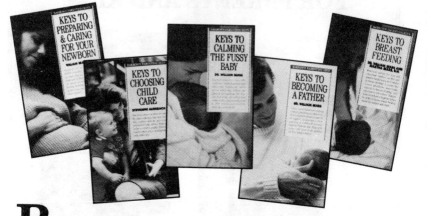